D0818651

WINNING LOTTO/ LOTTERY FOR EVERYDAY PLAYERS

To My family:
Ruby, Mac, Gary and Janice

About the Author

Prof. Jones is acknowledged as one of the leading designers of computer winning software for greyhound, standardbred, thoroughbred, lotto/lottery and sports betting in the world. His very powerful software products are considered to be on the cutting edge of technology by handicappers worldwide. The Prof. Jones' software line features more than 30 products on beating the odds.

With degrees in Psychology and Statistics, Prof. Jones has always been fascinated with the bias and randomness in numbers. He began his handicapping career in 1968, refining his betting skills at the Santa Anita and Hollywood Park race tracks, and in 1983, transformed this knowledge into the first thoroughbred computer software that actually produced consistent winners.

When lotteries and lottos became a national obsession, Prof. Jones applied his experience and knowledge of statistics to create the Gold and Platinum series Lotto/Lottery software programs for the everyday player. These successful and practical strategies are considered by many to be the most powerful winning systems ever designed for these games.

The basic theories of Prof. Jones outstanding programs have been simplified and incorporated into the easy-to-read winning strategies presented in this book. For serious lotto and lottery players looking to win more jackpots, the highly acclaimed and successful strategies advertised in the back of the book are highly recommended.

Other Books and Strategies by Prof. Jones

The Basics of Winning Lotto/Lottery
Master Lotto and Lottery Strategies
Pro Master II Lotto and Lottery Strategies
Five Ball Lotto Wheels
Winner's Guide to Greyhound Racing

WINNING LOTTO/ LOTTERY FOR EVERYDAY PLAYERS

Prof. Jones

- Gambling Research Institute -
CARDOZA PUBLISHING

CARDOZA PUBLISHING
Visit our web site! www.cardozapub.com

Cardoza Publishing is the foremost gaming and gambling publisher in the world with a library of almost 100 up-to-date and easy-to-read books and strategies. These authoritative works are written by the top experts in their fields and with more than 6,500,000 books in print, represent the best-selling and most popular gaming books anywhere.

Third Edition   *July 2002*

Library of Congress Catalog Card No: 2002101327
ISBN: 1-58042-047-8
Front Cover Photo by Ron Charles
Author Photo by Clint Broadbent

Write for your free full color catalogue of gambling books, advanced, and computer strategies.

CARDOZA PUBLISHING
PO Box 1500 Cooper Station, New York, NY 10276
Phone (718)743-5229 • Fax (718)743-8284
E-Mail: cardozapub@aol.com
www.cardozapub.com

TABLE OF CONTENTS

Hot Number Power Balls
High Frequency Power Balls
Frequency Power Ball Strategy
Hot Number Strategy
Combination Strategy Using Ties
Multiple Power Ball Strategy
Conclusion

12. Advanced Winning Methods 103
Skip/Hit Analysis
Creating a Skip/Hit Chart
Hot Numbers with High Frequency
Hot Numbers with Low Frequency
Cluster Analysis
Significant Cluster
Playing and Charting a Cluster
Regression Analysis

13. Key Numbers 115
Key Numbers
Positional Analysis Key Number
Positional and Hot Number
Key Number Wheels

14. Dream Analysis Strategy 119
Historical Overview of Dream Analysis
Psychology and Parapsychology
Why You Dream
Dream Symbolism
Associating Dreams with Numbers
Associating Numbers with Symbols
Strategy
Conclusion

15. Dimitrov Wheels 125

16. Computer Strategies 137
Introduction
Operating System
Lottery Software
The Optimizer

1. INTRODUCTION

Million dollar payoffs have tempted more people than ever to wager money on lotto and the lottery. Many rely on luck or random picks for their occasional winners, but in this book, we'll show you how to scientifically track and wheel numbers, so that you can swing the odds in your favor and be a winner!

While others rely on luck and waste their hard earned money playing lucky numbers and making bets involving little or no strategy, using our strategies, you'll be playing the best percentages and going for the big jackpots each time you play.

After you've finished reading this book, you'll never again have to depend on luck, because we'll show you how the use of our simple methods and strategies will substantially increase your chances of winning the big jackpots. In no time at all, you'll be playing and winning like a pro!

You'll learn how to get the best percentages and be a winner. We teach you everything from the 3 and 4-ball lottery strategies to beginning and advanced 6-ball wheeling systems, demonstrating many different winning approaches, from conservative to aggressive, and from beginning to expert.

You'll learn how to spot high and low frequency numbers and numbers that can win for you. Also, how to identify hot numbers and correctly bet them, and even how to create the same 6-ball wheels used by lotto experts worldwide.

WINNING LOTTO FOR EVERYDAY PLAYERS

There's lot's of proven winning information in this book, a book full of my inside tips, ready for you to use in going after the big jackpot that can give you financial freedom.

After you have read this book you will have the knowledge to play any lottery or lotto in the world. You will also have the power to dramatically increase your odds of winning and of becoming very wealthy!

2. A SHORT HISTORY OF THE GAME

When pre-historic man began to domestically raise grain, he immediately started fermenting it into something that made life more tolerable in the cave. Soon after that he devised games of chance which we have been play-ing ever since.

The existence of lotto dates as far back as 1530. The Italians called it "La Lotto de Firenze" and it was surprisingly similar to today's lotto.

Citizens purchased tickets and won prizes based upon a percentage of the total money collected. The state's share of the money was used to build roads, schools and other civic structures.

The game was so popular that it quickly spread throughout Europe. When the European settlers came to America they were used to playing the lotto at home so they created similar games in their new country. Most of these games were legal, but some were not.

In the past, illegal games were an integral part of big city life. Numbers were normally bet through "runners" and a portion of the pot was paid to the winners. The recent emergence of

legalized lotteries in almost every state has significantly reduced illegal lotteries because state run lotteries are easier to
bet and the payoffs are higher.

This book was written to provide winning techniques that can be
applied to all types of legal lotteries and lottos.

By using these simple techniques you will be able to make
wagers that are intelligent and have the best chance of winning!

3. INSTANT GAMES

When states first initiate their lotteries they normally begin with basic scratch-off **Instant Winner** tickets. There are literally hundreds of different gimmicks and prizes available. You simply purchase the ticket and scratch off a silver latex paint to see if you have won.

Some states even offer bonus winners the chance to win additional prizes by spinning a wheel or guessing numbers on TV. Although it is not possible to make a consistent profit playing the Scratch Off games we will still outline some simple strategies that should be used.

If you must play the Instant Game at least buy the tickets that promise the highest possible prize. Many states offer $1.00 tickets that guarantee one winner for every five tickets sold. A winning ticket pays a mere $5.00 but they claim your odds of winning are excellent! These tickets should definitely not be considered in your betting plans because the risk to reward ratio is too small.

The best strategy is to only purchase tickets that have a payoff of at least $10,000 or more. Even though the odds of winning are much lower than the $5.00 payoff mentioned in the previous paragraph, it really makes more sense to bet $1.00 trying to win $10,000, than to risk $1.00 on a top prize of only $5.00.

With enough said about the Instant Game, let's now learn how to use simple number tracking methods that will produce real profits in the 3 and 4-ball lottery, and the lotto.

4. UNDERSTANDING BIAS

Bias

An action or event is biased if it shows a consistent pattern over time. A pair of dice will always produce more sevens than twelves over an extended number of rolls because it is mathematically easier to roll a seven. But, if you add weight to each die on the side where the sixes are, this will adversely effect the normal pattern of numbers thrown. This added weight creates a **bias**.

When you look at all of the past numbers selected in your lottery you will notice that certain numbers are always drawn more frequently than other numbers. The reason this happens is because some type of a bias exists in either the balls or the holding bin they are drawn from. It occurs because all physical devices have differences.

One popular explanation for the existence of bias in lottery is that the numbers on balls contain different amounts of paint and therefore have a different weight. Another is that the air reaction to different number patterns causes the balls to rise at different rates.

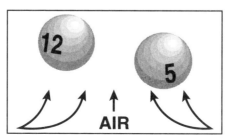

Despite what the lottery commission claims, randomness can never be totally achieved so there will always be some form of bias; and that is exactly what we are trying to exploit.

Using a Bias

A very good illustration of how a bias could be exploited would be if a roulette wheel had been built with a major defect. Suppose the black numbered slots were much deeper than the red numbered slots. Each time the wheel was spun, the ball would have a tendency to fall into the deeper black spaces and not come out. If you kept track of a large number of spins, the black numbers would always have a higher frequency than the red numbers.

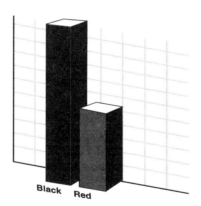

Black   Red

Figure 4.1 - Biased Distribution Graph

Figure 4.1 represents the results of several thousand spins on the defective wheel. As you can clearly see, the black numbers have a higher frequency than the red numbers. If you were betting this wheel, and had created a frequency chart of its results, you would probably play black over red and make a nice profit. This is exactly the same strategy that you will use for the lottery.

Lottery Bias

Lottery numbers are added to a frequency chart in a manner similar to the roulette wheel. This method is referred to as a **Frequency Analysis** and is used to isolate biases and show you exactly which numbers appear most often. Similar to the black numbers on the flawed roulette wheel, you will also play lottery numbers that have shown the highest frequency of occurrence.

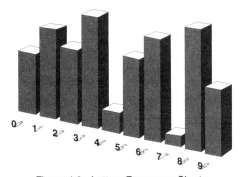

Figure 4.2 - Lottery Frequency Chart

In Figure 4.2 we have compiled a chart representing 500 four-ball lottery draws. The chart shows us that number **8** has the highest frequency of occurrence with number **3** second. Numbers **1**, **2**, **5** and **6** are also high frequency numbers and should be considered.

The best way to recognize biases is to keep track of frequency. The black numbers appeared more frequently on the roulette wheel because the factory accidentally made the black spaces deeper, thus creating a bias. This same Frequency Analysis can also be used to study lottery numbers.

Chapter 5 will show you how to profit from this knowledge.

5. WINNING THE LOTTERY

The popular three and four-ball lotteries are played almost daily in most states. Balls numbered from **0** to **9** are placed in individual bins or containers. Using forced air, balls are pushed one at a time into a tube located on top. When all of the balls are selected they become the daily number.

In the example below, number **368** was selected in the 3-ball game and number **7299** in the 4-ball game.

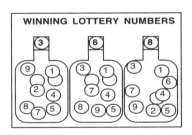

3   6   8
The winning number is 368

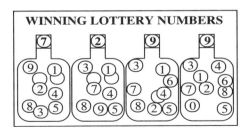

7   2   9   9
The winning number is 7299

It typically costs $1.00 per play for the lottery, with the payoff normally $500 for the "Pick Three" winner and $5000 for the "Pick Four" winner. This represents approximately one half of the total money bet.

Unlike the lotto, the lottery payoff always remains consistent. This is due to the volume of play and the fact that there will always be about the same number of winners each week. The pool may have less winners one week, and more the next, but it always averages out so prizes stay the same.

In lottery, the order that the balls are drawn is very important because they become an actual number. For us to analyze lottery it is necessary to reduce those numbers back into their original digits and sequence.

To make the analysis easier to understand, we will refer to each individual ball drawn as a **digit**, and the combination of the digits as a **number**.

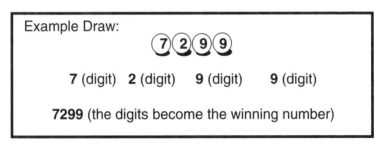

Example Draw:

7 (digit) 2 (digit) 9 (digit) 9 (digit)

7299 (the digits become the winning number)

The digits 7, 2, 9, and 9 make up the number seven-thousand, two-hundred and ninety-nine. (The concept of digit and number is extremely important throughout this entire lottery section so make sure you understand it.)

We study digits instead of numbers in the lottery because there are too many possible numbers. In 3-ball lottery the numbers range from 000 to 999. This means that you would have to follow 1000 possible numbers if you wanted to chart their frequency.

If all of the numbers were drawn, one per day, with no duplications, it would take 2.74 years before every one of the 3-ball combinations came up. The 4-ball numbers would take 27.4 years! The sheer volume makes it impossible to study the actual numbers. It is therefore necessary to study digits to predict future numbers.

Frequency Analysis
When you keep track of the frequency of occurrences, like you did on the roulette wheel in the previous chapter, it is referred to as *analyzing the frequency* or **Frequency Analysis**. In lottery, Frequency Analysis allows you to keep track of how often each digit was drawn so you can determine which digits are the most frequent.

In the simple frequency chart below we placed a dot next to the digit each time it was drawn. Number **8** was the most frequently drawn digit with number **6** coming in second.

FREQUENCY CHART

1	••••••••••••
2	•••••••
3	••••••••••••••••
4	•••••
5	••••••••••••••
6	•••••••••••••••••
7	•••••••••••••••
8	••••••••••••••••••
9	••••••••
0	•••

Figure 5.1 - Simple Frequency Chart

According to the sample data in Figure 5.1, numbers **3**, **5**, **6**, **7** and **8** should be included in your lottery bets because they have the highest frequency.

The problem with playing a simple Frequency Analysis is that it produces too many numbers to bet. In order to cover all possible combinations it would be necessary to include each number in each position. If you used all 5 lottery numbers, 625 combinations would be created. This is a lot of bets for the average person.

By using a Positional Analysis along with your Frequency Analysis, it is possible to substantially reduce the number of necessary bets because each position will also be analyzed.

Positional Analysis
Positional Analysis should represent the heart of your lottery strategy. It will allow you to keep track of the frequency of each number in each position drawn. This way you will not have to bet each digit in all positions, which we discovered could be very expensive.

The first step in creating a Positional Analysis is to correctly transfer your lottery numbers onto the chart. Each digit must be placed in its respective position.

The following examples represent three, 3 and 4-ball, lottery draws. The digits of the first 3-ball number (**745**) are transferred to their correct positions with **7** in the first, **4** in the second, and **5** in the third position.

Number **0926** in the 4-ball example is the first number to have its digits transferred to their correct positions. The digit **0** must be placed in the first position, digit **9** in the second , digit **2** in the third, and digit **6** in the fourth. All remaining numbers should have their digits transferred in the same manner.

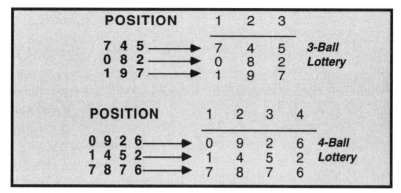

Examples of Placing Draws into Correct Positions

Now, transfer all of the digits onto a chart like Fig. 5.2 so they can be evaluated. The 3-ball chart has 3 columns because that is how many balls are drawn (745), and the 4-ball chart has 4 columns (0926).

Both charts have 10 rows down because there are 10 possible digits drawn in each position (0 through 9). Figure 5.2 represents a sample 3 ball and a 4-ball chart.

Notice in Figure 5.2 that we placed a dot in each correct position for every digit of each number drawn. Your chart should also look like this.

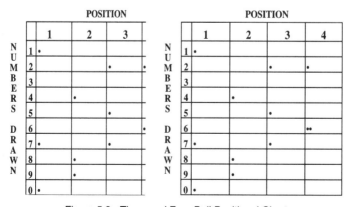

Figure 5.2 - Three and Four-Ball Positional Charts

After several months, your Positional Analysis chart will begin to show you exactly which numbers to play by illustrating the digits with the highest frequency in each position.

Figure 5.3 shows you how many times each number was drawn in each position. The chart below is how your chart will look after a large group of numbers is entered. We added up the dots and created the chart on the right so the figures would be easier to work with.

POSITION

NUMBERS DRAWN	1	2	3	4
1	4	2	6	5
2	2	3	4	5
3	6	5	10	6
4	3	1	3	5
5	5	5	1	5
6	5	5	6	5
7	3	8	4	2
8	9	4	2	4
9	10	6	3	4
0	3	3	2	10

Figure 5.3 - Positional Charts

POSITION

NUMBERS DRAWN	1	2	3	4
1	••••	••	••••••	•••••
2	••	•••	••••	•••••
3	••••••	•••••	••••• •••••	••••••
4	•••	•	•••	•••••
5	•••••	•••••	•	•••••
6	•••••	•••••	••••••	•••••
7	•••	••••••••	••••	••
8	••••• ••••	••••	••	••••
9	••••• •••••	••••••	•••	••••
0	•••	•••	••	••••• •••••

Figure 5.3 - Positional Charts

In this example, **9** is the most frequent digit in the first position, **7** in the second position, **3** in the third position, and **0** in the fourth position.

If you play the **9730** you are betting on the highest frequency digit in each position. This will provide you with the best chance of winning.

By studying the frequency in each position, rather than the overall frequency of each digit, you were able to reduce your number of bets from 625 to 1.

Advanced Lottery Strategy

Many lottery players prefer to bet more numbers in order to further increase their chances of winning. The Positional Analysis chart is an excellent way to decide which numbers to use. Instead of using just the highest frequency digit in each position, let's look at some other digits that are also good bets.

In the first position of Figure 5.4, the digits **3**, **8** and **9** have a high frequency. Digits **3**, and **7** are excellent in position two, digits **1**, **3** and **6** in position three, and **0** and **3**, must be considered in the last position.

NUMBERS DRAWN

POSITION			
1	**2**	**3**	**4**
4	2	6	5
2	5	4	5
6	6	10	6
3	1	3	5
5	5	1	5
5	5	6	5
3	8	4	2
9	4	2	4
10	5	3	4
3	3	2	10

Figure 5.4 - Positional Chart

As we mentioned earlier, it gets expensive when you play too many digits, but playing more than just the top frequency digits is good strategy. The next section contains the rules that should be used when deciding exactly which high frequency digits to play.

Rules For Selecting High Frequency Numbers

There are several rules that must be followed when choosing which top digits to take from the Positional Analysis chart and include in your bets.

In order to illustrate ties and other rules, charts similar to Figure 5.4 will be used as examples.

WINNING LOTTO FOR EVERYDAY PLAYERS

1. If you have two digits tied for the top pick, use only those digits, plus the second best digit (with ties) in your combinations.

POSITION

NUMBERS DRAWN	1	2	3	4
1	4	2	6	5
2	2	3	4	5
3	⑥	5	10	6
4	3	1	3	5
5	5	5	1	5
6	5	5	6	5
7	3	8	4	2
8	⑩	4	2	4
9	⑩	6	3	4
0	3	3	2	10

In this example the digits **8** and **9** would be used, plus the digit **3**. There were no other numbers that had six occurrences (like 3) so these are all of the numbers used for that position.

2. If there are three or more digits tied for the highest frequency, use only those digits for that position.

POSITION

NUMBERS DRAWN	1	2	3	4
1	4	2	6	5
2	2	3	4	5
3	6	5	10	6
4	3	1	3	5
5	⑩	5	1	5
6	5	5	6	5
7	3	8	4	2
8	⑩	4	2	4
9	⑩	6	3	4
0	3	3	2	10

In this example, the numbers **5**, **8**, and **9** all had ten occurrences and are used, but the number **3** (2nd choice) is left out.

3. If you have two or more digits tied for the second highest frequency in a position, use the highest and the second highest digit with ties.

POSITION

NUMBERS DRAWN	1	2	3	4
1	4	2	6	5
2	2	3	4	5
3	6	5	10	6
4	3	1	3	5
5	5	5	1	5
6	(9)	5	6	5
7	3	8	4	2
8	(9)	4	2	4
9	(10)	6	3	4
0	3	3	2	10

In this example, the top pick is the number **9**, and both **6** and **8** tied with the nine occurrences so these would be the only numbers used.

4. If you have any ties with the third highest frequency digit use only the top and second picks.

POSITION

NUMBERS DRAWN	1	2	3	4
1	4	2	6	5
2	2	3	4	5
3	5	5	10	6
4	3	1	3	5
5	5	5	1	5
6	5	5	6	5
7	3	8	4	2
8	(9)	4	2	4
9	(10)	6	3	4
0	3	3	2	10

In this instance, there are ties for third so only the top two numbers (8 and 9) are used in the analysis for that position.

In the first position of our Positional Analysis chart, figure 5.4, the digit with the highest frequency is **9**, the second highest frequency is **8** and the third highest frequency is **3**.

Digits with the highest frequency in the second position are the **7** and the **3**, with the **2**, **5**, **6** and **9** all tied for third. Since these ties do not involve the top pick, they will not be used in the analysis.

In the third position **3**, **6** and **1** are the top three picks. The **0** and **3** are the only digits used in the fourth position because several digits tied for third and therefore are not used in the analysis.

After using our rules, the numbers that qualify are as follows:

POSITION	1	2	3	4
NUMBERS	9	7	3	0
	8	3	6	3
	3		1	

Arrange the digits, similar to the example above, so you can easily create all of the possible combinations.

In order to list each combination of the digits that exhibited high frequency in each position, you start with the top line going left to right. Then you start from the fourth position and begin exchanging digits to form other combinations.

The most obvious number would be **9730**, this represents the highest frequency digit for each position assembled into a number.

POSITION	1	2	3	4
NUMBERS	**9**	**7**	**3**	**0**
	8	3	6	3
	3		1	

The next combination would be **9733**, all we did was exchange the **3** for the **0** in the last position.

POSITION	1	2	3	4
NUMBERS	**9**	**7**	**3**	0
	8	3	6	**3**
	3		1	

Remember, when creating your combinations always work from the fourth position to the first position.

You can now start using digits out of position 3 to create numbers.

POSITION	1	2	3	4
NUMBERS	**9**	**7**	3	**0**
	8	3	**6**	3
	3		1	

To follow, are all of the combinations using the first digit (**9**) along with the rest of the possible digits.

```
9730 9733 9760 9763 9710 9713
9330 9333 9360 9363 9310 9313
```

It is easy to create the remaining combinations. Simply change the digit in the first position and add the rest of the numbers. Remember, the top three digits for the first position were **9**, **8**, and **3**.

Let's now exchange the **9** with the **8** and use the exact same pattern for the rest of the number. This will create the second group of combinations.

```
9730 9733 9760 9763 9710 9713
9330 9333 9360 9363 9310 9313

8730 8733 8760 8763 8710 8713
8330 8333 8360 8363 8310 8313
```

Finally, substitute the **3** for the first number and do the same thing.

```
3730 3733 3760 3763 3710 3713
3330 3333 3360 3363 3310 3313
```

The 36 numbers below represent all combinations possible using the highest frequency digits from the Positional Analysis chart.

9730	9733	9760	9763	9710	9713
9330	9333	9360	9363	9310	9313
8730	8733	8760	8763	8710	8713
8330	8333	8360	8363	8310	8313
3730	3733	3760	3763	3710	3713
3330	3333	3360	3363	3310	3313

It will cost you $36 to play all of these numbers, but you will have a very good chance of winning the 4-ball lottery. If this seems expensive, there is one additional strategy that will provide you with almost as good a chance of winning but reduce the required wager.

Sum Total Analysis
If you study many lottery results it is apparent that the highest and lowest numbers (not digits) are rarely drawn. How often have you seen 0000 or 9999 picked? Sum Total Analysis allows you to easily identify and eliminate numbers that rarely appear before betting.

Target Range
To use sum total Analysis you add up each digit in each number and only play totals that fall into an acceptable range. This acceptable range is called the **Target Range**, and a Summation Chart is used to help find that exact range.

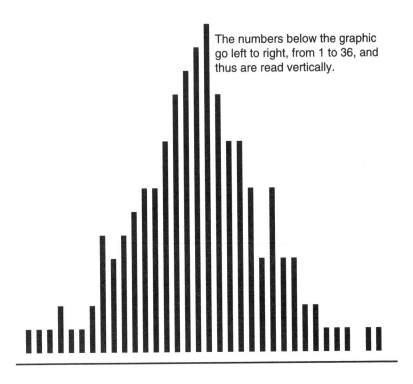

The numbers below the graphic go left to right, from 1 to 36, and thus are read vertically.

111111111122222222223333333
123456789012345678901234567890123456

Figure 5.5 - Four-Ball Lottery Sum Bell Curve

Figure 5.5 represents a typical sum Total Chart of 500 randomly selected 4-ball lottery numbers, which you can use to determine your Target Range. Sum totals of 0 through 8 had few occurrences along with sum totals of 30 through 36. This shows, without doubt, that very high and very low sum total numbers are rarely picked in the lottery.

Based upon this evidence it is suggested that you only play numbers with a sum total that falls within the target range shown to have a high probability. According to our chart, playable sum totals for the 4-ball lottery range from 15 through 23.

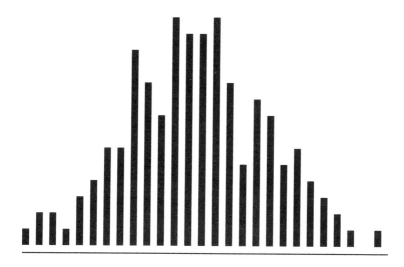

1111111111122222222
123456789012345678901234567

Figure 5.6 - Three-Ball Lottery Sum Bell Curve

The same method is used for the 3-ball lottery. Figure 5.6 represents a 3-ball sum total Chart using 500 numbers in a random draw. Sum total target ranges can be selected from this chart. Based on Figure 5.6, use sum totals from 9 through 19 for the 3-ball lottery.

How To Use The Summation Method
In order to figure out our best bets, let's use the **summation method** and add up each digit in each number. The first number was **9370** so the sum total is 19; 9 + 3 + 7 + 0. The second number was **9733** so the sum total is 22; 9 + 7 + 3 + 3. Each digit in each number is added up in this way.

For practice, let's do a sum total of all 36 numbers generated from the Positional Analysis earlier.

9730	9733	9760	9763	9710	9713
9330	9333	9360	9363	9310	9313
8730	8733	8760	8763	8710	8713
8330	8333	8360	8363	8310	8313
3730	3733	3760	3763	3710	3713
3330	3333	3360	3363	3310	3313

To the left are the 36 original plays generated by the Positional Analysis.

The *sum total* of each number must now be calculated.

9+7+3+0=19	8+7+3+0=18	3+7+3+0=13
9+7+3+3=22	8+7+3+3=21	3+7+3+3=16
9+7+6+0=22	8+7+6+0=21	3+7+6+0=16
9+7+6+3=25	8+7+6+3=24	3+7+6+3=19
9+7+1+0=17	8+7+1+0=16	3+7+1+0=11
9+7+1+3=20	8+7+1+3=19	3+7+1+3=14
9+3+3+0=15	8+3+3+0=14	3+3+3+0=09
9+3+3+3=18	8+3+3+3=17	3+3+3+3=12
9+3+6+0=18	8+3+6+0=17	3+3+6+0=12
9+3+6+3=21	8+3+6+3=20	3+3+6+3=15
9+3+1+0=13	8+3+1+0=12	3+3+1+0=07
9+3+1+3=16	8+3+1+3=15	3+3+1+3=10

As you can see, many of the numbers do not fall within the necessary range. Remove the ones that are outside the target range of 15 to 23.

9+3+3+3=18	8+7+3+0=18	8+3+1+3=15
9+7+3+3=22	8+7+3+3=21	3+7+3+3=16
9+3+1+3=16	8+3+3+3=17	3+7+6+0=16
9+7+6+0=22	8+7+6+0=21	3+7+6+3=19
9+7+1+0=17	8+7+1+0=16	3+3+6+3=15
9+7+1+3=20	8+7+1+3=19	
9+3+3+0=15	8+3+6+0=17	
9+7+3+0=19	8+3+6+3=20	

The remaining plays are in the target range and represent your bets.

Summary of Winning Lottery Techniques

In order to correctly analyze the lottery you must first use the Positional Analysis to show which numbers have the highest frequency in each position.

POSITION

NUMBERS DRAWN	1	2	3	4
1	• • • •	• •	• • • • • •	• • • • •
2	• •	• • •	• • • •	• • • •
3	• • • • • • •	• • • • •	• • • • • • • • • •	• • • • • •
4	• • •	•	• • •	• • • • •
5	• • • • •	• • • • •	•	• • • • •
6	• • • • • •	• • • • •	• • • • • •	• • • • •
7	• • •	• • • • • • • • • •	• • • •	• •
8	• • • • • • •	• • • •	• •	• • • •
9	• • • • • • • • • •	• • • • • •	• • •	• • • •
0	• • •	• • •	• •	• • • • • • • • • •

You then create the most probable combinations based on these high frequency numbers. Certain rules are followed to find the best number in case of ties (See pages 25-27).

9730	9733	9760	9763	9710	9713
9330	9333	9360	9363	9310	9313
8730	8733	8760	8763	8710	8713
8330	8333	8360	8363	8310	8313
3730	3733	3760	3763	3710	3713
3330	3333	3360	3363	3310	3313

Next use the Sum Total Chart to select a target range of totals that show a high frequency of occurrence. For the 3-ball lottery that range is between 9 and 19, and for the 4-ball it is between 15 and 23.

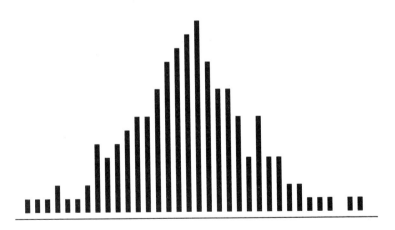

```
1111111111222222222233333333
12345678901234567890123456789012345456
```

By adding up each combination, picks are eliminated that fall outside the target range.

9+7+3+3=22	8+7+3+3=21	3+7+3+3=16
9+7+6+0=22	8+7+6+0=21	3+7+6+0=16
9+7+6+3=25	8+7+6+3=24	3+7+6+3=19
9+7+1+0=17	8+7+1+0=16	3+7+1+0=11
9+7+1+3=20	8+7+1+3=19	3+7+1+3=14
9+3+3+0=15	8+3+3+0=14	3+3+3+0=09
9+3+3+3=18	8+3+3+3=17	3+3+3+3=12
9+3+6+0=18	8+3+6+0=17	3+3+6+0=12

The remaining numbers represent the most strategic and productive bets possible for the 4-ball lottery example that was used.

9730	9733	9760	9710	9713
9330	9313	9333	8730	8733
8760	8710	8713	8333	8360
8363	8313	3733	3760	3763
		3363		

Conclusion

Using this simple statistical process you will be able to consistently cash tickets in the 3 and 4-ball lottery.

6. WINNING THE LOTTO

Introduction

The game that has captivated the minds of most Americans is the lotto. With payoffs as high as 100 million dollars for a single bet, players are always searching for any type of strategy that will increase their chances of winning.

The major downside to winning the lotto is the odds. If one single ticket is purchased, with no strategy or logic applied, the odds of winning are usually over 13,000,000 to 1. A common phrase repeated by many lotto players is, "Well, someone has to win." This certainly may be true, but that fact doesn't make it any easier for *you* to win.

In this section of the book you will first study the basics of the game, then you will learn the methods that will significantly increase your chances of winning.

The Game

Although each state has many variations of the lotto game, they are all actually very similar.

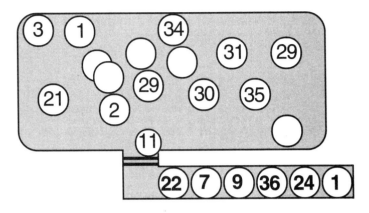

Lotto Game Bin

Balls (similar to ping-pong balls) are circulated in a bin and forced out into a holding tube by either air or gravity. These balls are numbered from 1 to whatever has been designated as the highest possible number, usually 49.

The standard format is the 6/49 lotto. This is a 6-ball draw that includes 49 possible numbers. Several states have recently initiated lottos that use over 50 balls. Some even draw a **bonus** ball which provides players with an extra chance to complete their 6-ball set.

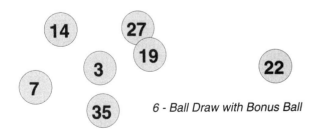

6 - Ball Draw with Bonus Ball

Differences Between the Lottery and Lotto

The two major differences between the lottery and the lotto are order of draw and the duplication of numbers.

1. Order of the Draw

In lottery the sequence of the draw actually creates a number.

Lottery balls drawn:

0   4   0   7

In this example the winning number is **0407**. The order of the draw was vitally important because it created the winning number.

Lotto balls drawn:

11   34   54   02   21   41

In the lotto example the order of the draw has no bearing on the outcome. In fact, the numbers are usually converted into ascending order when they are announced in the newspaper.

Below are the same numbers arranged in ascending (lowest to highest) order.

02   11   21   34   41   54

2. Duplicate Numbers

Due to the fact that 3 or 4 sets of the same 10 numbers are drawn in the lottery, duplications will often appear. Notice in our example how the digit **0** appears in position 1 and also 3.

0   4   0   7

Duplications are not possible in the lotto because a specified number of balls are drawn from only one bin.

Best Number Analysis

In the last chapter we discovered that the 3 ball lottery had 1000 possible numbers (000 to 999). The 4 ball had a whopping 10,000 (0000 to 9999). This made it impossible to create a Frequency Analysis for each number so the digits were analyzed instead.

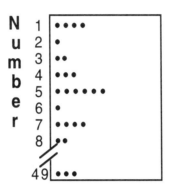

Figure 6.1 - Best Number Chart

In the lotto there are only 50 or so possible numbers so a Frequency Analysis of each number makes sense. Create a Frequency Analysis chart similar to Figure 6.1. The numbers 1 to 49 correspond to how many balls are selected in a typical lotto. If your lotto draws more balls, add more numbers to the chart. The dots represent each time a number was drawn.

Using this chart you will be able to observe the frequency of each number over a period of time. As you can see, the number **5** has the highest frequency with six occurrences, while numbers **2** and **6** have the fewest occurrences, appearing only one time each.

Playing the Frequency Chart

If you decide to use only the Frequency Analysis for your lotto strategy, simply keep track of the highest frequency numbers and play them. Numbers that have a high frequency over a long period of time are always a good bet.

Similar to the lottery, I strongly suggest that a Positional Analysis be used in conjunction with your Frequency Analysis. It will show you the highest frequency numbers as well as which position they are in.

Positional Analysis

The Positional Analysis chart is created in the same manner that it was in the lottery. The major difference is that there are more columns and rows. Columns represent the number of balls selected (6) in each draw and rows represent the actual balls (49). (See figure 6.2.)

Create a chart similar to this chart so you can easily place dots in the correct position each time a number is drawn.

To get acquainted with the lotto Positional Analysis, let's chart three winning draws from a sample 6/49 lotto. Remember, before any number is entered into the Positional Analysis, it must first be sorted into ascending order (lowest to highest). Below are the raw numbers in the exact order that they were drawn.

01	22	19	09	16	49
05	11	02	08	27	28
19	07	06	08	21	40

The same numbers are now sorted into ascending order.

01	09	16	19	22	49
02	05	08	11	27	28
06	07	08	19	21	40

Numbers that exhibit a high frequency are easy to spot in the positional charts on the following pages because there will always be more dots in the box. Like the Positional Analysis Chart used earlier in the lottery section, you are looking for the highest frequency numbers in each position.

POSITION

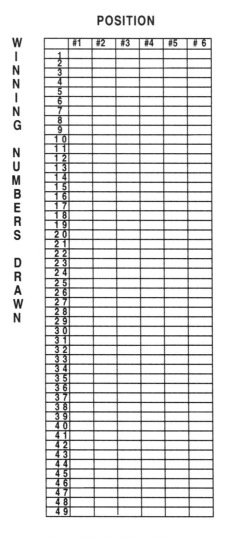

Figure 6.2 - Positional Chart

Numbers that exhibit a high frequency are easy to spot in the positional charts on the following pages because there will always be more dots in the box. Like the Positional Analysis Chart used earlier in the lottery section, you are looking for the highest frequency numbers in each position.

POSITION

	#1	#2	#3	#4	#5	# 6
1	•					
2	•					
3						
4						
5		•				
6	•					
7		•				
8			• •			
9		•				
1 0						
1 1				•		
1 2						
1 3						
1 4						
1 5						
1 6			•			
1 7						
1 8						
1 9				• •		
2 0						
2 1					•	
2 2					•	
2 3						
2 4						
2 5						
2 6						
2 7					•	
2 8						•
2 9						
3 0						
3 1						
3 2						
3 3						
3 4						
3 5						
3 6						
3 7						
3 8						
3 9						
4 0						•
4 1						
4 2						
4 3						
4 4						
4 5						
4 6						
4 7						
4 8						
4 9						•

Figure 6.3 - Positional Chart with Several Draws

Figure 6.3 shows your numbers entered into the correct boxes.

POSITION

WINNING NUMBERS DRAWN	#1	#2	#3	#4	#5	#6
1	●●●●●●					
2	●●●●●● ●●●●					
3	●●●●	●●●●●●				
4	●●●●● ●●●	●●●				
5	●●●●●●	●●●●●●	●			
6	●●●●	●●●	●●			
7	●●	●●●●●●	●●			
8	●●	●●●●●●	●●	●		
9	●●	●●●●●●	●●	●		
10		●●●●	●●●●	●	●	
11	●	●●●	●●●●●●			
12	●●		●●●●	●		
13		●●	●	●●●		
14	●	●●●●●●	●●●●	●●		
15		●●●	●●●●	●		●
16	●●		●●	●●		
17		●●●●●●	●●●	●		
18		●	●●●●	●●●		
19		●●	●●	●●●●●●	●●	
20			●●●●●			
21			●●	●	●●●●	
22			●●	●●●	●●●	
23			●●●	●●●●	●●●	
24				●●●●	●●	●
25				●●	●●●●	●
26			●	●	●●●●●	●
27				●●●●	●●●	●●
28				●	●●●●	●●●●
29					●●●●	●●
30					●●●●●	●●
31					●●●●●	●●●●●●
32				●	●●●●●●	●●●●●
33					●●	●●●●●
34						●●●●●●
35					●	●●●●●
36					●	●●●●●●
37						●●●
38				●		●●
39					●●●	
40					●●	
41					●●	●
42						●●●
43						
44					●	●●
45						●●
46						
47						●●
48						●
49						●●●

Figure 6.4 - Positional Analysis Chart with Many Draws

Remember, each time the winning numbers become available, place a dot in the correct box on your chart. Soon it will look like Figure 6.4.

POSITION

W I N N I N G N U M B E R S D R A W N	#1	#2	#3	#4	#5	# 6
1	5					
2	10					
3	4	6				
4	9	3				
5	5	6	1			
6	4	3	2			
7	2	6	2			
8	2	6	2	1		
9	2	6	2	1		
10		4	4	1	1	
11	1	3	6			
12	2		4	1		
13		2	1	3		
14	1	6	4	2		
15		3	4	1		1
16	2		2	2		
17			7	3	1	
18		1	4	3		
19		2	2	7	2	
20				5		
21			2	1	4	
22			2	3	3	
23			3	4	3	
24				4	2	1
25				2	4	1
26			1	1	5	1
27				4	3	2
28				1	4	4
29					4	2
30					5	2
31					5	6
32				1	6	5
33					2	5
34						8
35					1	7
36					1	6
37						3
38				1		2
39					3	
40					2	
41					2	1
42						3
43						
44					1	2
45						2
46						
47						2
48						1
49						3

Figure 6.5 - Numeric Positional Chart

All of the dots in each cell have been added up in Figure 6.5. This will make the chart easier to understand and analyze in the next section.

7. WINNING WITH POSITIONAL ANALYSIS

How to Use the Positional Analysis Chart
The same procedures will be used for the lotto Positional Analysis that were used for the lottery when selecting which numbers to bet.

Conservative players should play only the very highest frequency numbers with ties. Aggressive players should play the highest and second highest frequency numbers along with ties. This strategy will allow those players to cover more strategic numbers and greatly increase their chances of winning.

Aggressive players should also use the same rules explained earlier in the Lottery section (chapter 5) to choose which numbers to play. The rules define exactly which numbers must be included in all bets.

Rules For Using The Positional Analysis
1. If there are two numbers tied for the top pick, use those numbers plus the second best number (with ties) in your combinations.

2. If there are three or more numbers tied for the top number use only those numbers for that position.

3. If you have two or more numbers tied for the second highest number in a position, use the highest frequency and the second ties.

4. If you have any ties with the third highest frequency number use only the top and second picks, disregarding third ties.

Using Figure 6.5 (page 47) and the rules explained above, let's determine which numbers to include in our combinations.

Position #1
Number 2 has the highest frequency with 10 occurrences.
Number 4 has the second highest frequency with 9 occurrences.
Numbers 1 and 5 are tied and will not be used (rule 4).

Position #2
Numbers 3, 5, 7, 8, 9, and 14 are all tied for the highest frequency and therefore will be the only numbers used for that position (rule 2).

Position #3
Number 17 has the highest frequency with 7 occurrences.
Number 11 is the second highest frequency with 6 occurrences.
Numbers 10, 12, 14, 15 and 18 all have 4 occurrences and therefore will not be used (rule 4).

Position #4
Number 19 has the highest frequency with 7 occurrences.
Number 20 has the second highest frequency with 5 occurrences.
Numbers 23, 24 and 27 are all tied with 4 occurrences and will not be included (rule 4).

Position #5

Number 32 has the highest frequency with 6 occurrences. Numbers 26, 30, and 31 all have 5 occurrences and therefore will be included (rule 3).

Position #6

Number 34 has the highest frequency with 8 occurrences. Number 35 has the next highest frequency with 7 occurrences. Numbers 31 and 36 are tied with 6 occurrences and therefore will not be used (rule 4).

Below are the <u>high</u> frequency numbers that were selected from the Positional Chart using the rules. They are the numbers that should be used by aggressive players wanting more action.

2	3	17	19	32	34
4	5	11	20	26	35
	7			30	
	8			31	
	9				
	14				

Conservative players should play only the very highest frequency numbers listed below.

2	3	17	19	32	34
	5				
	7				
	8				
	9				
	14				

In this example, 6 numbers tied for the highest frequency in the second position. A tie involving this many numbers in a single position is considered abnormal, but let's learn how to deal with it.

Conservative players have two choices, they can pick one of the numbers from the second position to make a single combination, or use all of the ties to create 6 combinations.

Below is an example of how the bet would look if only number **3** was chosen for position two. This would create 1 combination.

| 2 | **3** | 17 | 19 | 32 | 34 |

Below are the combinations if ties were included in position two. (This does not represent every possible combination of all 11 numbers.)

2	**3**	17	19	32	34
2	**5**	17	19	32	34
2	**7**	17	19	32	34
2	**8**	17	19	32	34
2	**9**	17	19	32	34
2	**14**	17	19	32	34

Duplicate Numbers In Several Positions

When entering numbers into your Positional Analysis chart it is normal to have the same number appear in more than one position. If you look at the two draws below, you can see why.

Two 6-Ball Lotto draws:

02	**06**	21	23	43	49
06	19	28	31	36	44

As you can see in the example draws, the number **6** appeared in position #2 in the first draw and also in position #1 in the second draw. A Positional Analysis chart will contain many instances of this.

These duplicate numbers will have no effect on the wheels unless the same number is in several top positions. If a double occurrence exists, a good strategy is to use the next highest frequency number in that position to complete your wheel.

Example of a Double Occurrence:

2	3	17	**19**	32	34
4	5	**19**	20	26	35
	7			30	
	8			31	
	9				
	14				

The number **19** was one of the highest frequency numbers in both position 3 and 4. When you create your combinations, use number **17** for position three and number 19 for position four.

Example of a Tie for the Top Position:

2	3	19	19	32	34
		17			

The highest frequency numbers include a duplication (number

19) so number **17** would also be used to complete the bet for players that only play the highest frequency numbers.

Wheeling Numbers

When you create your actual bets you must create 6-ball combinations if it is a 6-ball lotto. This process is often referred to as **wheeling numbers** or creating "betting combinations."

Below is a combination using only your highest frequency sample numbers. This combination represents a very conservative bet that only costs $1.00.

If you decide to wheel all of the numbers, so as to create every possible combination, it would take a large number of bets.

Number of numbers.	Number of combinations.
6	1
7	7
8	28
9	84
10	210
11	462
12	924
13	1716

The chart reveals that the number of possible combinations is very high even with a minimal amount of numbers. If you included all 18 of the original numbers generated from the Positional Analysis chart for aggressive players, it would require 18,564 bets to cover every possible combination!

Even if you only used the conservative top numbers with ties (11 numbers), and wanted all of the possible combinations, it would still require 462 bets. (On page 52 we did not create every possible combination of all 11 numbers, we only placed ties in position #2.)

Before you decide that the game is too expensive for your taste, see chapter 9 which deals with Abbreviated wheeling systems and sum total analysis. These powerful strategies will substantially reduce the number of plays necessary to win.

8. PLAYING THE ODDS

Understanding The Odds

Most people who purchase lotto tickets do not comprehend the actual odds. Instead they only focus on the possibility of winning millions of dollars while rarely incorporating any strategy or logic. This allows professional players, who are themselves acutely aware of the odds, to gain a distinct advantage over the rest of the field.

These professionals apply a simple formula to calculate the odds of winning the lotto. This same formula can be used for any number of total balls and balls drawn.

$$\frac{49}{6} \qquad \frac{49 \times 48 \times 47 \times 46 \times 45 \times 44}{6 \times 5 \times 4 \times 3 \times 2 \times 1} = 13{,}983{,}816$$

The formula illustrates that there are 13,983,816 possible 6 ball combinations in a 49 ball pool. Therefore, if you play a single combination in a 6/49 lotto your odds of winning the top prize is 13,983,816 to 1.

You can use this same formula to calculate the odds of winning a lotto that contains a different number of total and selected balls. Simply insert the total number of balls on top, and the number of balls that are drawn on the bottom. The formula below is for a 6/39 lotto and it demonstrates that the odds of winning are 3,362,623 to 1 for a single combination.

39	$\frac{39 \times 38 \times 37 \times 36 \times 35 \times 34}{6 \times 5 \times 4 \times 3 \times 2 \times 1}$ =	3,362,623
6		

Secondary Prizes

Considering the high odds, it would be extremely difficult to realize a profit in the lotto if only 6 ball winners were rewarded. The good news is that there are payoffs for as few as 3 correct balls out of your 6 ball combinations, and these secondary prizes are also much easier to hit. Secondary prizes not only generate income, but more importantly, provide you with capital to continue your quest for the top prize.

Below is a chart that illustrates the odds of winning various prizes in several different games. It must be noted that even though the odds of winning are exact, the payoff is always dependent upon the actual number of winning tickets.

Game	1st Prize ODDS = 6/6	2nd Prize ODDS = 5/6	3rd Prize ODDS = 4/6	4th Prize ODDS = 3/6
6/49	13,983,816	54,201	1,032	57
6/48	12,271,512	48,696	950	53
6/44	7,059,052	30,961	669	42
6/42	5,245,786	24,286	555	37
6/40	3,838,380	18,816	456	32
6/39	3,362,623	16,478	412	30

Figure 8.1 - Odds (to 1) Of Winning Prizes

According to this chart your odds of winning a secondary prize are actually quite good, especially if the numbers you play are selected using the proven strategies outlined in this book.

Creating A Bet

When you establish your actual bets, you must create 6-ball combinations if it is a 6-ball lotto. This process is often referred to as creating betting **combinations**.

Following is a single combination using only your highest frequency sample numbers from the Positional Analysis. This combination represents a very conservative bet that only costs $1.00.

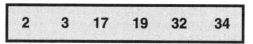

Considering that most strategies generate more than 6 numbers, you must now learn how to create the additional combinations necessary to include these numbers.

Creating Complete Wheels

If you want to include additional numbers within your bet you must create more advanced combinations. **Wheeling** refers to the method used to incorporate more than 6 numbers into these combinations.

There are two types of wheels, **complete** and **abbreviated**. A wheel is considered complete when it contains all possible combinations of the original numbers that were used to create the wheel. This means that regardless of which six numbers are selected in the lotto, if they are contained in the original numbers that you wheeled, you win. Abbreviated wheels do not contain all of the possible combinations and will be covered in the following chapter.

A simple way to learn how a wheel is created would be to add another number to your previous 6 ball combination. Anytime you want to play over 6 numbers the numbers must be wheeled. To create a complete wheel with 7 numbers requires playing 7 combinations instead of just one. This way all possible combinations are included in the bet.

Below are the numbers that you will include in the wheel.

Original bet						Additional Number
2	3	17	19	32	34	5

The easiest method to wheel numbers is to use a template. Figure 8.2 represents the template used to wheel 7 balls into 7 individual combinations or bets. This template is read vertically, up and down, with the first combination represented by 1-2-3-4-5-6. It is important to note that templates are not the actual numbers that you are going to bet, but instead represent the order used when creating your bets. (This will be explained in greater detail in the chapter on Dimitrov wheeling systems.

1	1	1	1	1	1	2
2	2	2	2	2	3	3
3	3	3	3	4	4	4
4	4	4	5	5	5	5
5	5	6	6	6	6	6
6	7	7	7	7	7	7

Figure 8.2 - Template For Complete 7 Ball Wheel

In order to create the actual bets, you must match the seven numbers that you want included in the wheel (your numbers), with the numbers in the template. Number 5 is being used as the seventh number because it was previously identified as a tie in the second position of the Positional Analysis.

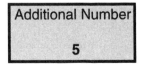

Original bet						Additional Number
2	3	17	19	32	34	5

First arrange your numbers into ascending (lower to higher) order prior to placing them into the template.

2	3	5	17	19	32	34

Now place your numbers directly underneath the 7 boxes so they can easily be transposed. There are 7 boxes because you are wheeling 7 numbers.

01	02	03	04	05	06	07
02	03	05	17	19	32	34

Finally, substitute your seven high frequency numbers with the numbers on the template and this will give you a complete wheel of the combinations. For example, wherever the 07 shows, you place the 34 number, and wherever the 05 shows, you place the 19. This is shown below.

01	02	03	04	05	06	07
02	03	05	17	19	32	34

02	02	02	02	02	02	03
03	03	03	03	03	05	05
05	05	05	05	17	17	17
17	17	17	19	19	19	19
19	19	32	32	32	32	32
32	34	34	34	34	34	34

Figure 8.3 - Actual Bets On Template

Your actual combinations are constructed vertically in the template. You can now arrange them horizontally so they are visually easier to interpret.

Bet							
	1	02	03	05	17	19	32
	2	02	03	05	17	19	34
	3	02	03	05	17	32	34
	4	02	03	05	19	32	34
	5	02	03	17	19	32	34
	6	02	05	17	19	32	34
	7	03	05	17	19	32	34

Although your overall bet increased to $7, your chances of hitting the 6 ball winner also increased seven times! This occurred because each one of the 7 combinations are unique, causing your overall odds of winning to increase proportionally.

To calculate these new odds simply divide 13,983,816 by 7. By using this simple wheel your odds have now improved to 1,997,688 to 1!

6/49 Single Bet Odds	6/49 Complete Wheel Odds (7 Ball)
13,983,816 to 1	1,997,688 to 1

The advantage of using complete wheeling systems is that you are guaranteed to win the 6 ball lotto regardless of which balls are drawn, as long as they are included in the balls that you used to create the wheel.

The disadvantage of complete wheeling systems becomes apparent when even more numbers are added to your wheel. Wheeling all combinations becomes very expensive.

Figure 8.4 shows just how costly playing complete wheels can be if you use an abundance of numbers.

Total Number of Balls	Possible Combinations	Total Number of Balls	Possible Combinations
6	1	28	376,740
7	7	29	475,020
8	28	30	593,775
9	84	31	736,281
10	210	32	906,192
11	462	33	1,017,568
12	924	34	1,344,904
13	1,716	35	1,623,160
14	3,003	36	1,947,792
15	5,005	37	2,324,784
16	8,008	38	2,760,681
17	12,376	39	3,262,623
18	18,564	40	3,838,380
19	27,132	41	4,496,388
20	38,760	42	5,245,786
21	54,265	43	6,096,454
22	74,613	44	7,059,052
23	100,947	45	8,145,060
24	134,596	46	9,366,819
25	177,100	47	10,737,573
26	230,230	48	12,271,512
27	296,010	49	13,983,816

Figure 8.4 - Cost Of Playing Complete Wheels

The chart reveals that there are a large number of possible combinations even with a minimal amount of numbers. If you included all 18 of the original numbers generated from the Positional Analysis chart for aggressive players, it would require 18,564 bets to cover every possible combination!

Even if you only used the conservative top numbers with ties (11 numbers), and wanted all of the possible combinations, it would still require 462 bets. (On page 52 we did not create every possible combination of all 11 numbers, we only placed ties in position #2.)

Before you decide the game is too expensive for your taste, the next section of this book shows you how to create Abbreviated Wheeling Systems which will substantially reduce the number of plays necessary to make you a winner.

9. DIMITROV WHEELING SYSTEMS

Basic Dimitrov Theory

Dimitrov was a famous mathematics professor who lived in Austria. He developed the **Dimitrov Abbreviated Wheeling Systems**. These wheeling systems are still used by many advanced lotto players.

The systems provide a good chance of winning without the need to bet every possible combination. They are referred to as *abbreviated systems* because not every possible combination is created. The advantage of using a Dimitrov system is that it allows you to play all of your high frequency numbers at a very reasonable cost .

Dimitrov's Abbreviated Wheeling Systems also provide a **confidence level**, or *assurance of winning* for each wheel. This confidence level guarantees that when a certain number of your balls appear in the draw, there will always be at least one winning combination.

Before we proceed, let's look at the three factors that must be considered when choosing which Dimitrov wheel to use.

1. Numbers Wheeled: This relates to how many numbers you want included in the wheel. The high frequency digits in the Positional Analysis example earlier produced 18 numbers, so a Dimitrov wheeling system that utilizes 18 numbers should also be used. Or if you use 10 numbers, make sure the wheeling system utilizes 10 numbers.

2. **Combinations Created**: This relates to how many combinations or bets will be created from the wheel. Each wheel is different. Light bettors should choose wheels that produce 6 or less bets. Aggressive bettors can create wheels that produce over 60 bets.

3. **Confidence Level**: This relates to how many of your balls must appear in the draw in order for you to have a win. It also determines if the win will be a 3, 4 or 5 ball win. The *minimum assurance of win* guarantees that you will get at least one win, and maybe more, if the minimum number of your balls are drawn.

Dimitrov Wheeling System #59 was designed for 18 numbers and produces 15 plays (bets), so we will use it as an example.

According to its confidence level, if five balls are drawn out of the original 18, you have the assurance of getting at least one 3-ball winner. This is a good wheel for the average player to use.

18/15

1	1	1	1	1	2	2	2	2	3	3	3	7	9	10
2	3	4	4	4	5	5	5	6	6	6	6	8	12	11
3	7	7	8	14	7	8	13	8	7	8	9	10	13	13
4	9	10	9	15	9	11	15	10	10	11	12	11	14	15
5	12	13	11	17	10	14	16	13	14	13	15	15	16	17
6	14	16	12	18	12	17	18	15	17	16	18	18	17	18

Figure 9.1 - Dimitrov System #59

Creating a Dimitrov Wheel

Dimitrov wheeling systems are really only *templates* that are used to hold your numbers. These templates are designed to accept an exact amount of numbers, and produce the same number of bets each time. Figure 9.2 illustrates Dimitrov System #27, which is designed to produce 6 combinations (bets) from 11 numbers. The combinations or bets produced are to be read vertically.

11/6

1	1	1	1	1	6
2	2	2	2	2	7
3	3	3	3	3	8
4	4	4	4	4	9
5	5	5	5	5	10
6	7	8	9	10	11

Figure 9.2 - Dimitrov System #27

Each combination includes 6 numbers (top to bottom). But, as mentioned earlier, this is only the template that accepts the numbers you want to play, not the actual numbers. Let's create a Dimitrov wheel using the 11 highest frequency numbers that were previously generated from the Positional Analysis chart on page 47.

Chosen and System Numbers
Numbers that you want to wheel are always referred to as **chosen numbers**. These chosen numbers can be generated from the Positional Analysis or any other method of analysis. Chosen numbers are simply the numbers that you choose to play.

Numbers that make up the Dimitrov template are called the **system numbers**. System numbers are only a guideline, they are never part of the actual bet. System numbers must always be replaced by the chosen numbers. This creates the combinations that you bet.

The first step is to select the Dimitrov wheeling system that you want to use to wheel your numbers with. Use the three factors outlined earlier in this chapter. The system below produces 6 bets from the 11 chosen numbers.

11/6

1	1	1	1	1	6
2	2	2	2	2	7
3	3	3	3	3	8
4	4	4	4	4	9
5	5	5	5	5	10
6	7	8	9	10	11

Figure 9.3 - Dimitrov System #27

These are the system numbers in Dimitrov #27. Remember, these numbers are only a template designed to hold your chosen numbers.

Four Guessed Numbers = 3-Number Wins

System	01	02	03	04	05	06	07	08	09	10	11
Chosen											

Figure 9.4 - Number Bar

Each of the chosen numbers must first be placed in the **number bar** before they can be transferred to the Dimitrov System #27 template. Place the 11 highest frequency numbers including ties into the number bar so that you know exactly where they need to go on the template. The number bar contains exactly 11 boxes for the 11 highest frequency numbers we are using as our chosen numbers.

Four Guessed Numbers = 3-Number Wins

System	01	02	03	04	05	06	07	08	09	10	11
Chosen	02	03	05	07	08	09	14	17	19	32	34

Figure 9.5- Dimitrov System #27 with System and Chosen Numbers

Always make sure that your chosen numbers are in ascending order (lowest to highest) before you place them into your number bar. Now, replace the system numbers in the template on the left with their corresponding chosen number (shown in the number bar) into the template on the right. Chosen number 2 replaces system number 1, chosen number 3 replaces system number 2, and so on until all system numbers are replaced by chosen numbers.

11/6

1	1	1	1	1	6
2	2	2	2	2	7
3	3	3	3	3	8
4	4	4	4	4	9
5	5	5	5	5	10
6	7	8	9	10	11

11/6

2	2	2	2	2	9
3	3	3	3	3	14
5	5	5	5	5	17
7	7	7	7	7	19
8	8	8	8	8	32
9	14	17	19	32	34

Figure 9.6 - Dimitrov System #27 with System and Chosen Numbers

Your actual bets for System #27 are:

02	02	02	02	02	09
03	03	03	03	03	16
05	05	05	05	05	17
07	07	07	07	07	19
08	08	08	08	08	32
09	14	17	19	32	34

For aggressive players let's create even more bets by using system #59 and all 18 high frequency numbers with ties. The number bar must contain 18 boxes because you will be using the 18 high frequency numbers generated earlier from the Positional Analysis.

Five Guessed Numbers = 3-Number Wins

System	01	02	03	04	05	06	07	08	09	10	11	12	13	14	15	16	17	18
Chosen	02	03	04	05	07	08	09	11	14	17	19	20	26	30	31	32	34	35

Figure 9.7 - Dimitrov System #59 Number Bar with Chosen Numbers

When your chosen numbers replace the Dimitrov system numbers the bets are generated. (See Figure 9.1 on page 66 for system numbers.)

18/15

2	2	2	2	2	3	3	3	3	4	4	4	9	14	17
3	4	5	5	5	7	7	7	8	8	8	8	11	20	19
4	9	9	11	30	9	11	26	11	9	11	14	17	26	26
5	14	17	14	31	14	19	31	17	17	19	20	19	30	31
7	20	26	19	34	17	30	32	26	30	26	31	31	32	34
8	30	32	20	35	20	34	35	31	34	32	35	35	34	35

Figure 9.8 - Dimitrov System #59 substituted with Chosen Numbers

These are your actual bets:

```
02 03 04 05 07 08
02 04 09 14 20 30
02 05 09 17 26 32
02 05 11 14 19 20
02 05 30 31 34 35
03 07 09 14 17 20
03 07 11 19 30 34
03 07 26 31 32 35
03 08 11 17 26 31
04 08 09 17 30 34
04 08 11 19 26 32
04 08 14 20 31 35
09 11 17 19 31 35
14 20 26 30 32 34
17 19 26 31 34 35
```

Chapter 15, Dimitrov Wheels, contains Dimitrov wheeling templates that can be used to wheel any combination of numbers that you desire. Conservative players can use the wheels that produce less plays.

Even more Dimitrov wheeling templates are available in the Advanced Strategies described in the back of this book.

Lotto Sum Total Analysis

Similar to the lottery, the Sum Total Analysis is also a good strategy when analyzing the lotto. Through the use of Sum Total Analysis you will be able to eliminate totals that are either too high or too low. Totals that are not in the target range rarely appear and therefore should not be played.

Combinations are added up in the same manner that they were in the lottery. Each number in the combination becomes part of the sum total.

Below is a combination from the 11-ball wheel.

Numbers Added:	**2 3 5 7 8 9** **2+3+5+7+8+9=34**

The sum total of the combination is 34.

For the purpose of illustration, let's use all 11 numbers representing the highest frequency numbers from the Positional Analysis Chart. They have previously been wheeled using System #27, which produced 6 combinations.

Each combination must now be added.

2	2	2	2	2	9
3	3	3	3	3	14
5	5	5	5	5	17
7	7	7	7	7	19
8	8	8	8	8	32
+ 9	+ 14	+ 17	+ 19	+ 32	+ 34
34	**39**	**42**	**44**	**57**	**125**

As you can see, the sum totals for the six wheeled numbers range from 34 to 125 (the first five numbers are abnormally small because of the tie).

Figure 9.9 represents a Sum Total Chart that contains 500 complete draws in the 6/49 lotto. According to this chart, a sum total range of 98 to 209 represents the target range, since it contains the bulk of the draws. Even though the most frequent sums were 152, 158 and 173, it is not necessary to concern yourself with individual high frequency sums. You will use the target range to find the best combinations.

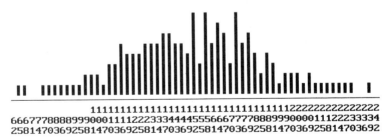

Figure 9.9 - 500 Game Lotto Sum Bell Curve

When using sum totals it is necessary to use a Dimitrov wheeling system that produces an adequately large number of wheeled combinations, so that when the high and low totals are removed a reasonable number of bets will still remain.

2	2	2	2	2	9
3	3	3	3	3	14
5	5	5	5	5	17
7	7	7	7	7	19
8	8	8	8	8	32
+ 9	+ 14	+ 17	+ 19	+ 32	+ 34
34	39	42	44	57	125

It is obvious in this sample that system #27 is productive only if you desire a single bet. The sixth column contains the one combination that fits into our target range by having a sum total of 125. All of the other totals are too small.

In the original Positional Analysis, 6 small numbers tied for the highest frequency in position 2, causing most of the combinations in this wheel to contain such small sum totals that they are out of the 98 to 209 target range represented in Figure 9.9.

2	3	17	19	32	34
	5				
	7				
	8				
	9				
	14				

It is unusual for there to be this many ties for the highest frequency, therefore even smaller wheels will typically produce a larger percentage of playable combinations that fall within the target range.

This example contains only the very highest frequency numbers with ties and uses a wheeling system that produces only 6 plays. To produce more plays, more combinations must be initially generated. Many will be outside the target range and therefore will not be used.

It is also important to understand that when you apply the Sum Total Analysis to Dimitrov wheeling system results, you change the standard confidence level. The *assurance of winning* is no longer exactly the same, because you reduced part of the wheel by not wagering on numbers outside the target range.

I suggest that you will have a better chance of winning by starting with larger wheels and throwing out totals that are too high or low, even if it changes the confidence level. This procedure produces the most productive wagers possible. Combinations that fall outside the target range should not be played.

Let's perform a Sum Total Analysis on the 18 high frequency numbers that were previously generated in our Positional Analysis. We will use Dimitrov System #59 which produces 15 combinations out of 18 chosen numbers.

18/15

2	2	2	2	2	3	3	3	3	4	4	4	9	14	17
3	4	5	5	5	7	7	7	8	8	8	8	11	20	19
4	9	9	11	30	9	11	26	11	9	11	14	17	26	26
5	14	17	14	31	14	19	31	17	17	19	20	19	30	31
7	20	26	19	34	17	30	32	26	30	26	31	31	32	34
8	30	32	20	35	20	34	35	31	34	32	35	35	34	35

Figure 9.10 - Dimitrov System #59

We must now do a Sum Total Analysis of all 15 combinations in order to eliminate the ones that are not in the target range.

1	2	3	4	5	6	7	8	9	10	11	12	13	14	15
2	2	2	2	2	3	3	3	3	4	4	4	9	14	17
3	4	5	5	5	7	7	7	8	8	8	8	11	20	19
4	9	9	11	30	9	11	26	11	9	11	14	17	26	26
5	14	17	14	31	14	19	31	17	17	19	20	19	30	31
7	20	26	19	34	17	30	32	26	30	26	31	31	32	34
+8	+30	+32	+20	+35	+20	+34	+35	+31	+34	+32	+35	+35	+34	+35
29	79	91	71	137	70	104	134	96	102	100	112	122	156	162

The sum totals range from 29 in column 1 to 162 in column 15. According to the 6/49 Sum Total Chart in Figure 9.9, the target range is 98 to 209. This means that the combinations in columns 5, 7, 8, 10, 11, 12, 13, 14 and 15 all qualify. The bets that qualify are:

02	05	30	31	34	35
03	07	11	19	30	34
03	07	26	31	32	35
04	08	09	17	30	34
04	08	11	19	26	32

04	08	14	20	31	35
09	11	17	19	31	35
14	20	26	30	32	34
17	19	26	31	34	35

As you can see, it is necessary to use a wheeling system that initially produces more plays than you want to bet because the Sum Total Analysis will reduce your actual plays by an average of 35%.

Summary of Winning Lotto Techniques

In order to correctly analyze the lotto, you first use the Positional Analysis Chart to select numbers with the highest frequency of occurrence in each position. Rules for ties are similar to the ones used in the lottery.

2	3	17	19	32	34
4	5	11	20	26	35
	7			30	
	8			31	
	9				
	14				

You then create the most probable combinations of the high frequency numbers using a Dimitrov wheeling system.

02 03 04 05 07 08
02 04 09 14 20 30
02 05 09 17 26 32
02 05 11 14 19 20
02 05 30 31 34 35
03 07 09 14 17 20
03 07 11 19 30 34
03 07 26 31 32 35
03 08 11 17 26 31
04 08 09 17 30 34
04 08 11 19 26 32
04 08 14 20 31 35
09 11 17 19 31 35
14 20 26 30 32 34
17 19 26 31 34 35

Five Guessed Numbers = 3-Number Wins

System	01	02	03	04	05	06	07	08	09	10	11	12	13	14	15	16	17	18
Chosen	02	03	04	05	07	08	09	11	14	17	19	20	26	30	31	32	34	35

18/15

2	2	2	2	2	3	3	3	3	4	4	4	9	14	17
3	4	5	5	5	7	7	7	8	8	8	8	11	20	19
4	9	9	11	30	9	11	26	11	9	11	14	17	26	26
5	14	17	14	31	14	19	31	17	17	19	20	19	30	31
7	20	26	19	34	17	30	32	26	30	26	31	31	32	34
8	30	32	20	35	20	34	35	31	34	32	35	35	34	35

After that you analyze the Sum Total Chart to select a target range of sums with an acceptable frequency of occurrence. For a 6-ball, 49 number lotto, the target range would be between 98 and 209.

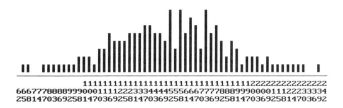

```
                    111111111111111111111111111111111222222222222222222
            666777888889990001111222333444455566677778888999000011122233334
            2581470369258147036925814703692581470369258147036925814703692
```

By adding up each combination, you then use the Sum Total Analysis to eliminate any combinations that are outside the target range previously determined by the Sum Total Chart.

2	2	2	2	2	3	3	3	3	4	4	4	9	14	17
3	4	5	5	5	7	7	7	8	8	8	8	11	20	19
4	9	9	11	30	9	11	26	11	9	11	14	17	26	26
5	14	17	14	31	14	19	31	17	17	19	20	19	30	31
7	20	26	19	34	17	30	32	26	30	26	31	31	32	34
+8	+30	+32	+20	+35	+20	+34	+35	+31	+34	+32	+35	+35	+34	+35
29	79	91	71	137	70	104	134	96	102	100	112	122	156	162

The remaining combinations represent the most strategic and productive bets possible for the lotto example that was used.

02	05	30	31	34	35
03	07	11	19	30	34
03	07	26	31	32	35
04	08	09	17	30	34
04	08	11	19	26	32

04	08	14	20	31	35
09	11	17	19	31	35
14	20	26	30	32	34
17	19	26	31	34	35

Conclusion

These steps and analyses will enable you to always place the most logical bets in your lotto game and greatly increase your winnings!

10. FIVE BALL LOTTO

Introduction

Many states now offer lotto games that select 5 balls instead of 6, and include 40 or less numbers in the pool. These 5-ball games often have catchy names, like "Pot Of Gold" or "Fantastic 5," and are often touted as being superior to traditional 6/49 lotto games because they are easier to win.

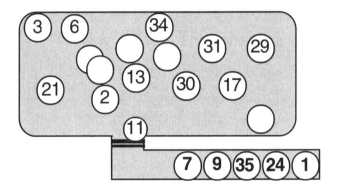

Figure 10.1 - Lotto Game Bin

Pick 5 games are easier to win than Pick 6 simply because fewer balls are drawn out of a smaller pool. In a typical game, 5 balls are drawn out of a total pool of 35 numbers. This game is often referred to as a 5/35 and is similar, but not necessarily superior to a 6/49.

The major difference between 6/49 and 5/35 lotto games involves the method of payoff. Many 5/35 games offer a *fixed* top prize that is unrelated to the actual odds or amount of money in the betting pool, while most 6/49 games offer *variable* prizes that are dependent on these two factors.

This chapter compares the relationship between odds and payoffs in both fixed prize and variable prize games in order to illustrate the positive and negative characteristics. By understanding how to evaluate a lotto, you will be able to choose games that offer the best return.

Odds Of Winning A 5/35

Before playing any lotto you might want to calculate the actual odds of winning. Knowing a game's odds or difficulty allows you to determine what a reasonable payoff should be.

The odds of winning a 5/35 lotto can be calculated using a formula similar to the one illustrated in Chapter 8. The only difference between these two formulas are the number of balls drawn and the total pool.

Odds For 5/35 Lotto

$$\frac{35}{5} \qquad \frac{35 \times 34 \times 33 \times 32 \times 31}{5 \times 4 \times 3 \times 2 \times 1} = 324{,}632 \text{ to } 1$$

According to the formula, the odds of winning a 5/35 lotto are 324,632 to 1 for a single bet.

Odds In Relation To Payoff

With the exception of Power Ball, odds of winning should never be a factor when determining whether a lotto game is worthy of your investment. Odds of winning *in relation to payoff* is what really counts. It is acceptable to play lotto games with very high odds (13,000,000 to 1 or higher) if the payoff or top prize reflects those odds.

For example, a lotto with odds of 13,000,000 to 1 should offer top prizes in the $3,000,000 to $5,000,000 range to qualify as playable. Games that are easier to win, like the 5/35, should still provide top prizes relative to their odds in order to be considered a good bet.

Example Of Odds In Relation To Payoff

It is necessary to understand the relationship between odds and payoff before you can select the best lotto game to play. By examining a common 3 and 4 ball lottery this relationship will become apparent and can later be applied to the lotto.

A standard 4-ball lottery has a top prize of $5,000 based on odds of 10,000 to 1. This top prize represents 50% of all the money wagered and is paid to players that successfully pick 4 numbers in correct order.

Figure 10.2 - 4-Ball win pays 50%

The odds of winning a Pick 3 lottery are 1,000 to 1 because you only need to predict 3 numbers. The Pick 3 lottery is therefore 10 times easier to win than the Pick 4.

Figure 10.3 - 3-Ball win pays 50%

Considering that the Pick 3 pays a top prize of $500, or 50% of the total money wagered, the payoff is equivalent to the Pick 4. This means both games provide identical payoffs in relation to odds.

Let's pretend for a moment that the Pick 3 only offered a top prize of $250 or 25%. The game would still be 10 times easier to win than the Pick 4, but the payoffs relative to the odds would obviously not be as good. Under these circumstances the 3-ball payoff would represent only 50% of the 4-ball payoff - just 25% - and is therefore a poor bet regardless of the superior odds.

Figure 10.4 - 3-Ball win pays 25%

Whether you are deciding to invest your money in a 6/49, 5/35 or any other form of lottery or lotto, you must always evaluate the payoff in relation to the odds in order to determine which games are best to play.

Prize Distribution In Lotto Games

A variable prize lotto represents how a payoff is derived as a percentage of the betting pool. This type of lotto payoff is standard in the 6/49 and other recommended games.

In a variable prize lotto, approximately 55% of the total money wagered is retained by the state and vendors, with the remaining money paid back to players in the form of prizes. The top prize is always highly publicized and accounts for the lion's share of the pool. It is calculated by adding up the total amount of money in the prize pool (minus a minimal amount to cover secondary prizes) and dividing by the number of winning tickets.

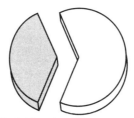

Figure 10.5 - Variable prize Lotto pays 35% to 40%

The top prize pool in a variable prize lotto is normally between 35% to 40% of the total prize pool. Remember, the entire prize pool represents about 45% of the total money wagered because 55% was initially retained by the state.

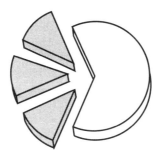

Figure 10.6 - Multiple prize winners share pool

If more than one correct ticket exists, top prize money is split equally among the winning ticket holders. If a single person holds duplicate tickets that contain the winning numbers, and no other winning tickets exist, that person wins no more than one ticket would have produced.

Playing tickets with identical number combinations in a variable prize lotto obviously makes no sense.

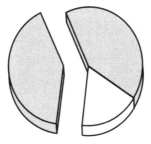

Figure 10.7 - Example of carryover expanding pool

Carryover is another nice feature of most variable prize lotto games and occurs when there are no top prize winners for a particular drawing. The money designated to pay the top prize is added to the top prize pool in the next drawing. This substantially increases the top prize pool and creates those 100 million dollar payoffs that keep players coming back.

Prize Distribution In 5/35 Lotto Games
Unlike variable prize lottos, some 5/35 lotto games offer fixed top prizes that pay a specified amount of money. These top prizes remain constant regardless of how much money is in the pool or the number of winning tickets. Considering that this method of payoff is very different than the variable prize payoffs previously discussed, 5/35 payoffs must be evaluated very closely before these games are played.

The possibility of multiple winners forces fixed prizes to be set low. The only way a top prize can be guaranteed is if that prize represents a very small percentage of the total money wagered. If the guaranteed top prize was similar to a variable prize lotto, and represented 35% to 40% of the pool, the lotto would lose money with multiple winners. In order to insure that a game with fixed prizes always makes a profit, the payoff must be very low in relation to the odds.

Top prize payoffs for 5/35 games typically pay $25,000 to $35,000. According to the odds, out of every 324,632 tickets sold, there should be 1 winning combination. Under this arrangement, the lotto can afford 4 to 6 top winners per draw and still realize a profit of over 50% because top prize money represents 10% or less of the pool. Even if there are no winners, the top prize remains the same. Carryover does not exist in fixed prize games.

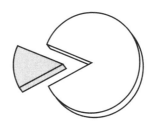

Figure 10.8 - 10% fixed top prize in 5/35 Lotto

Although $35,000 may seem like a lot of money to the average person, it is actually far less than the odds suggest. Considering that the odds of winning are 324,632 to 1, a payoff of 10% or less of the total money wagered is paltry in comparison with the 35% to 40% in a variable prize game. Add to this the lack of carryover and a 5/35 fixed prize game loses its appeal. Contrary to what many 5-ball promoters say, better odds do not always make a better game.

In order for a 5/35 game to be playable, it should provide a top prize that constitutes at least 35% to 40% of the total money wagered. Since this cannot be accomplished with fixed prize payoffs, these games should be avoided.

Pick Five Strategy
Once you have determined that the payoff is acceptable, playing a Pick 5 is actually easier than a Pick 6 because there are less balls. You can also use strategies similar to ones previously outlined in this book to isolate the best numbers and provide winning combinations.

Positional Analysis
Positional Analysis is recognized as the most powerful tool in any lotto analysis and should be used as the basis of your 5-ball strategy. I suggest also using the Skip/Hit Chart and Cluster Analysis to isolate additional numbers that can also be included in your wheels.

Figure 10.9 represents the 5-Ball Positional Analysis chart used to identify the most frequent numbers in each position. Notice there are 5 columns instead of the standard 6 as illustrated in Chapter 6.

POSITION

W		#1	#2	#3	#4	#5
I	1					
N	2					
N	3					
I	4					
N	5					
G	6					
	7					
N	8					
U	9					
M	10					
B	11					
E	12					
R	13					
S	14					
	15					
D	16					
R	17					
A	18					
W	19					
N	20					
	21					
	22					
	23					
	24					
	25					
	26					
	27					
	28					
	29					
	30					
	31					
	32					
	33					
	34					
	35					

Figure 10.9 - 5-Ball Positional Analysis Chart

Use the exact same procedures previously demonstrated in the 6-ball strategy when filling in the 5-ball Positional Analysis chart.

POSITION

	#1	#2	#3	#4	#5
1	5				
2	10				
3	7	6			
4	9	3			
5	5	6	1		
6	4	3	2		
7	2	6	2		
8	2	6	2	1	
9	2	6	2	1	
10		4	4	1	1
11	1	3	6		
12	2		4	1	
13		2	1	3	
14	1	6	4	2	
15		3	4	1	
16	2		2	2	
17			7	3	1
18		1	4	3	
19		2	2	7	2
20				5	
21			2	1	4
22			2	3	3
23			3	4	3
24				4	2
25				2	4
26		1		1	5
27				4	3
28				1	4
29					4
30					5
31					5
32				1	6
33					2
34					
35					1

W
I
N
N
I
N
G

N
U
M
B
E
R
S

D
R
A
W
N

Figure 10.10 - Positional Analysis Chart with Numbers

After the Positional Analysis Chart is filled with totals, you are ready to create betting combinations. This is accomplished by wheeling the numbers using complete or abbreviated systems.

Complete Wheel For 5-Ball Lotto

When you play a complete wheel you are assured of a 5-ball hit regardless of which 5 balls are drawn, as long as they are included in your chosen numbers. The simplest complete wheel contains 5 chosen numbers and creates a single bet. In this example the chosen numbers represent the top five numbers taken from the Positional Analysis Chart.

2	3	17	19	32
4	5	11	20	26
	7			30
	8			31
	9			
	14			

System	01	02	03	04	05
Chosen	02	03	17	19	32

02	03	17	19	32

This bet cost $1.00 and insures a 5-ball winner if all 5 chosen balls are selected.

Complete Wheels With Multiple Chosen Numbers

You will often have ties in your Positional Analysis or want to wheel additional numbers from other strategies. To accomplish this, you need a wheel that allows for more than 5 chosen numbers.

Below is a complete wheel that incorporates 6 chosen numbers and creates every permutation of these numbers. The number 5 was a tie in Position 2 of the Positional Analysis and therefore will be used as the sixth number in the wheel.

2	3	17	19	32
	5			
	7			
	8			
	9			
	14			

System
Chosen

01	02	03	04	05	06
02	03	05	17	19	32

1	1	1	1	1	2
2	2	2	2	3	3
3	3	3	4	4	4
4	4	5	5	5	5
5	6	6	6	6	6

These are the actual combinations that you bet.

2	2	2	2	2	3
3	3	3	3	5	35
5	5	5	17	17	17
17	17	19	19	19	19
19	32	32	32	32	32

This bet costs $6.00 and includes 6 balls in 6 combinations. If any 5 of the 6 chosen balls are drawn, you are guaranteed a 5-ball winner.

Abbreviated Wheels For 5-Ball Lotto
Most 5-ball players use abbreviated wheeling systems instead of complete wheeling systems in order to play more numbers.

The Dimitrov wheeling systems referred to earlier in this book are not designed to handle 5-ball wheels. This makes it necessary to create abbreviated wheels that accomplish the same task while still wheeling only 5 numbers.

One nice feature of 5-ball abbreviated wheels is that they are able to offer an *assurance of winning* similar to Dimitrov wheels. This assurance guarantees a specified win (4-ball, 3-ball etc.) contingent upon a minimum number of chosen balls being drawn.

7/9 Combination Wheel - 4-Ball Assurance
Below is a 5-ball abbreviated wheeling system that produces 9 wheels out of 7 chosen numbers and assures at least one 4-ball winner if 4 chosen numbers are correct.

Our 7 chosen numbers will include the highest frequency Positional Analysis numbers, plus #5 and #7 which represent ties in column 2.

System	01	02	03	04	05	06	07
Chosen	02	03	05	07	17	19	32

1	1	1	1	1	1	1	2	3
2	2	2	2	2	2	4	4	4
3	3	3	3	3	3	5	5	5
4	4	4	5	5	6	6	6	6
5	6	7	6	7	7	7	7	7

These are the actual combinations that you bet.

2	2	2	2	2	2	2	3	5
3	3	3	3	3	3	7	7	7
5	5	5	5	5	5	17	17	17
7	7	7	17	17	19	19	19	19
17	19	32	19	32	32	32	32	32

This wheel assures you a second place (4-ball) win if any 4 of the 7 chosen numbers are selected.

7/9 Combination Wheel- 3- Ball Assurance

The following example is another 7 chosen number wheel that only requires 5 combinations and assures at least one 3-ball win, if 3 winning numbers are selected out of the chosen 7.

System	01	02	03	04	05	06	07
Chosen	02	03	05	07	17	19	32

1	1	1	1	2
2	2	3	4	3
3	5	5	5	4
4	6	6	6	5
7	7	7	7	6

These are the actual combinations that you bet.

2	2	2	2	3
3	3	5	7	5
5	17	17	17	7
7	19	19	19	17
32	32	32	32	19

The same number of chosen balls are used in this wheel as were used in the previous wheel, but the assurance guarantees a 3-ball hit instead of a 4.

Additional 5-Ball Wheels - Assorted Assurance Levels

Eight additional 5-ball wheels providing varied assurances and number of chosen balls are included in the following section.

Five Guessed Numbers = 5-Number Wins

System	01	02	03	04	05	06
Chosen						

#1: 6/6

```
1 1 1 1 1 2
2 2 2 2 3 3
3 3 3 4 4 4
4 4 5 5 5 5
5 6 6 6 6 6
```

Five Guessed Numbers = 5-Number Wins

System	01	02	03	04	05	06	07	08
Chosen								

#2: 7/21

```
1 1 1 1 1 1 1 1 1 1 1 1 1 1 1 2 2
2 2 2 2 2 2 2 2 2 2 3 3 3 3 4 3 3
3 3 3 3 3 3 4 4 4 5 4 4 4 5 5 4 4
4 4 4 5 5 6 5 5 6 6 5 5 6 6 6 5 5
5 6 7 6 7 7 6 7 7 7 6 7 7 7 7 6 7
```
```
2 2 2 3
3 3 4 4
4 5 5 5
6 6 6 6
7 7 7 7
```

Four Guessed Numbers = 4-Number Wins

System	01	02	03	04	05	06	07	08	09
Chosen									

#1: 9/30

```
1 1 1 1 1 1 1 1 1 1 1 1 1 2 2 2 2 2
2 2 2 2 2 2 2 3 3 3 3 4 4 3 3 3 3 4
3 3 3 4 4 5 5 4 4 5 5 5 5 4 4 5 5 5
4 6 8 6 7 6 7 6 7 6 7 6 8 6 7 6 7 6
5 7 9 8 9 9 8 9 8 8 9 7 9 9 8 8 9 7
```

```
2 3 3 3 3 3 3 1 2 3 4 5
4 4 4 4 4 4 4 6 6 6 6 6
5 5 5 5 5 5 5 7 7 7 7 7
8 6 6 6 7 7 8 8 8 8 8 8
9 7 8 9 8 9 9 9 9 9 9 9
```

Five Guessed Numbers = 4-Number Wins

System	01	02	03	04	05	06	07	08	09	10	11
Chosen											

#2:11/26

```
1  1  1  1  1  1  1  1  1  1  2  2  2  2  2  2  2  2
2  2  2  2  3  3  3  4  4  6  3  3  3  3  4  4  5  5
3  4  6  8  4  6  9  5  5  7  4  4  5  5  6  7  6  7
8  5  7  9  5  7 10  6  9  9  6  7  6  7 10  9  9 10
10 8  8 11 10 10 11  7 11 11  9 11 11  9 11 10 10 11
```

```
3  3  3  3  4  4  5  5
4  4  5  5  6  7  6  7
6  7  6  7  8  8  8  8
8  8  8  8  9 10 10  9
11 9  9 11 10 11 11 10
```

93

Three Guessed Numbers = 3-Number Wins

System	01	02	03	04	05	06	07	08	09	10	11
Chosen											

#1: 8/8

```
1  1  1  1  1  2  3  4
2  2  2  2  5  5  5  5
3  3  3  3  6  6  6  6
4  4  4  4  7  7  7  7
5  6  7  8  8  8  8  8
```

#2:9/12

```
1  1  1  1  1  1  1  2  2  2  3  3
2  2  2  2  3  4  5  3  4  4  4  5
3  3  3  4  5  7  6  4  5  5  6  6
4  6  8  6  7  8  8  7  6  7  7  7
5  7  9  8  8  9  9  9  9  9  8  8  9
```

#3:10/17

```
1   1   1   1   1   1   1   1   2   2   2   2   3   3   3   4   6
2   2   2   2   3   3   3   4   3   3   4   5   4   4   5   6   7
3   4   5   6   4   5   5   5   4   5   6   6   5   6   6   7   8
6   7   8   7   8   7   9   6   5   7   9   8   7   8   7   8   9
9   9  10   8   9  10  10  10   8  10  10   9   9  10   8  10  10
```

#4:11/21

```
1   1   1   1   1   1   1   1   1   1   2   2   2   2   2   2   3   3
2   2   2   2   4   4   4   6   6   8   4   4   4   5   5   5   4   4
3   3   3   3   5   5   5   7   7   9   6   7   7   6   6   7   6   6
4   6   8  10   6   8  10   8  10  10   9   8   9   8   9   8   8   9
5   7   9  11   7   9  11   9  11  11  11  11  10  11  10  10  11  10
```
```
3   3   3
4   5   5
7   6   7
8   8   9
10  10  11
```

11. INTRODUCTION TO POWER BALL

Power Ball has quickly become the most intriguing game in town, providing both the largest payoff and greatest challenge for winning. At first glance, Power Ball and standard 6 Ball lotto appear to be similar, but a closer examination reveals that the odds of winning are actually quite different. Upon completion of this chapter you'll not only understand how to calculate the odds on Power Ball, but will also know the most effective strategies for winning.

Understanding The Game
The term **Power Ball** can refer to either the sixth ball drawn (the actual Power Ball), or the game as a whole. Power Ball will be referred to both ways in this chapter, depending solely on the context in which the term is used.

Power Ball actually consists of two separate lotto games rolled into one. It is similar to a five ball lotto and a one ball lotto combined into a single draw. Five balls are drawn from the first pool and then the sixth ball is drawn from the second pool. What makes the odds of winning the Power Ball substantially higher is that the sixth ball is drawn from a pool containing all of the possible numbers, rather than the reduced pool found in traditional 6/49 games.

Power Ball games typically have more than 50 balls for the 5 ball portion of the draw and another 50 plus balls for the Power Ball itself. Like the 6/49, a total of 6 balls are drawn, but the game and odds of winning are very different. This is partially due to the additional balls, but the most important difference is the way they are drawn.

Calculating Power Ball Odds

All of the numbers in the 6/49 lotto are drawn from the same pool. What this means is that each time a ball is drawn, less balls remain for the next draw, thus increasing the probability that your balls will be selected. (In other words, the *fewer the balls* remaining the easier it is to win because there are *less possible balls* available to be drawn.)

This concept is reflected in the formula used to calculate the odds of the 6/49 lotto. Each time a ball is drawn the top multiplier is reduced by 1. The final number 44 represents the remaining number of balls left in the pool that are available for the last draw.

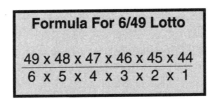

$$\text{Formula For 6/49 Lotto}$$

$$\frac{49 \times 48 \times 47 \times 46 \times 45 \times 44}{6 \times 5 \times 4 \times 3 \times 2 \times 1}$$

As you can see from the Power Ball example below, the first five balls are drawn from a pool of 50 balls in a manner similar to the 6/49 lotto. After each ball is drawn, one less ball remains in the pool.

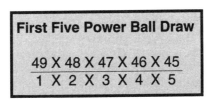

$$\text{First Five Power Ball Draw}$$

$$\frac{49 \times 48 \times 47 \times 46 \times 45}{1 \times 2 \times 3 \times 4 \times 5}$$

Even though the initial 5 ball draw is done in exactly the same way as a standard lotto, the difference between Power Ball and a conventional 6/49 lotto is that after the first five balls have been drawn, there are still 50 balls remaining for the last pick, rather than the usual 44.

This occurs because the Power Ball is selected from its own separate pool. To the average player this may not seem like a big difference, but let's see how it actually affects your chances of winning.

In Chapter 8, you learned how to calculate the odds for the 6/49 lotto. According to the formula your odds of picking the winning combination with a single bet was 13,983,816 to 1. Below is the formula used to calculate the odds of picking the correct six Power Ball numbers. This includes the five balls drawn out of the first pool and the Power Ball drawn out of the second pool. The formula is similar to the one used for the 6/49 lotto except their are 50 total balls and the sixth ball or Power Ball is selected from 50 balls rather than the normal reduced pool.

Power Ball Draw Using 50 balls:

$$\frac{50 \times 49 \times 48 \times 47 \times 46 \times 50}{5 \times 4 \times 3 \times 2 \times 1 \times 1} = \frac{12,712,559,616}{120} = 105,938,000 \text{ to } 1$$

Notice that instead of the last two multipliers being 45 and 6, like they were when you applied the standard lotto formula, they are 50 and 1. This occurs because the last draw is the Power Ball which is drawn out of a separate pool of 50 balls. The natural odds of winning the Power Ball is 105,938,000 to 1, as apposed to 13,983,816 to 1 for a standard 6/49 lotto. As you might have already suspected, you will have to learn some real strategy to play this game with any success.

Power Ball Strategy

The preferred strategy to use when playing Power Ball is to treat it as a combination 5 ball and a 1 ball lotto when analyzing the numbers. Use the Positional Analysis outlined in Chapter 7 for the five ball part of the pick, and either a Frequency Analysis or Hot Number Analysis to isolate the sixth ball.

Picking The Five Balls

The following example contains numbers that were generated using a five ball Positional Analysis. This analysis is essentially the same as the six ball Positional Analysis (see Chapter 7), only it's minus one ball. After you have kept track of the first five balls drawn in the Power Ball, isolate the best numbers in each position along with any ties.

| 2 17 19 32 34 | Best Numbers |

These are the numbers that you will include in the five ball portion of your Power Ball combination.

POSITION

		#1	#2	#3	#4	#5
W	1	6				
I	2	10				
N	3	7	6			
N	4	9	3			
I	5	6	6	1		
N	6	4	3	2		
N	7	2	6	2		
	8	2	6	2	1	
I	9	2	6	2	1	
N	10		4	4	1	1
G	11	1		6		
	12	2		4	1	
	13		2	1	3	
N	14	1	6	4	2	
U	15		3	4	1	
M	16	1		2	2	
	17		7	7	3	1
M	18		1	4	3	
B	19		2	8	7	2
E	20				5	
	21			2	1	4
R	22			2	3	3
S	23			3	4	3
	24				4	1
	25				2	4
	26			1	1	5
D	27				4	3
R	28				1	4
A	29					5
	30					6
W	31				1	3
	32				9	2
N	33					
	34					8
	35					

Picking The Power Ball
Now that you have isolated the correct numbers to use in the first part of your combination, the next step is to identify your sixth ball or Power Ball. Using a Frequency Analysis play either high frequency numbers or hot numbers for the Power Ball.

Hot Number Power Balls
Power Ball numbers that are the most overdue, meaning that they have not been drawn for the longest period of time, are referred to as **Hot Numbers**. These Hot Numbers can be easily isolated by using a standard Skip/Hit chart (see Chapter 12).

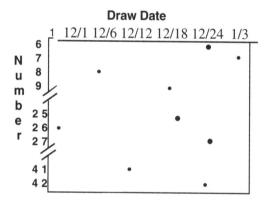

Skip/Hit Chart

In the chart above, we see that the most overdue number is 26, followed by 8 and 41.

High Frequency Power Balls
A **Frequency Analysis** will isolate Power Ball numbers that have been drawn most frequently in the past. High frequency numbers have a tendency to be drawn in the future and, therefore, are a good bet.

Frequency Power Ball Strategy

Using this strategy you create a single combination using the High Frequency number.

1	····················
2	························
3	·····················
4	·······················
5	····························
6	··································
7	·························
8	······················
9	···················
10	················
11	·················
12	·····················
13	····················
14	·····························
15	·····················
16	······················
17	·························
18	···················
19	············
20	············
21	······················
22	··················
23	·····················
24	·················
25	···············
26	···········
27	············
28	·················
29	···················
30	···············
31	················
32	···················
33	···················
34	·························
35	······························

Frequency Analysis

According to the Frequency Analysis, number 6 had the highest frequency, with number 14 and 35 finishing second.

2 17 19 32 34	Best Five Numbers
6	Highest Frequency Power Ball
2 17 19 32 34 **6**	Combination

Hot Number Strategy

In this strategy you will create a single combination using the Hot Number.

2 17 19 32 34	Best Numbers
26	Hot Number Power Ball
2 17 19 32 34 **26**	Combination

Combination Strategy Using Ties

If you have a tie in the five number Positional Analysis, it can be used to create multiple combinations.

2 17 19 32 34	Best Number
8	Tie
6	Designated Power Ball
2 17 19 32 34 **6**	Combination
8 17 19 32 34 **6**	Combination
2 8 19 32 34 **6**	Combination
2 8 17 32 34 **6**	Combination
2 8 17 19 34 **6**	Combination
2 8 17 19 32 **6**	Combination

Multiple Power Ball Strategy

It is also possible that you will include more than one Power Ball in your combinations. This will happen when you have several High Frequency or **Hot** Power Ball numbers that you want to be included with your best 5 balls. The following are examples of how to do this.

Best 5 ball picks	High Frequency Numbers
2 17 19 32 34	(6) (14) (35)
First Combination	2 17 19 32 34 (6)
Second Combination	2 17 19 32 34 (14)
Third Combination	2 17 19 32 34 (35)

Best 5 ball picks	Hot numbers
2 17 19 32 34	(8) (26) (41)
First Combination	2 17 19 32 34 (8)
Second Combination	2 17 19 32 34 (26)
Third Combination	2 17 19 32 34 (35)

Unlike 6/49 lotto, it is even possible to have duplicate numbers in a Power Ball combination.

Best 5 ball picks	Power Balls
5 12 21 34 44	17 43 44
First Combination	5 12 21 34 44 (17)
Second Combination	5 12 21 34 44 (43)
Third Combination	5 12 21 34 44 (44)

Notice that the number 44 appears twice in the third combination. This could not happen if you were playing a standard 6/49 lotto because it is impossible for numbers to be selected twice out of the same pool. Power Balls are selected from a second pool so it is possible that they may duplicate one of the first five balls.

Conclusion
Though I have shown you strong playing strategies, my suggestion is to stay clear of Power Ball because the odds aren't as good as a standard 6-ball game.

I recommend that you play the standard 6-ball lotto using the strategies outlined in this book. You have a much better chance of cashing winning tickets and making all of the money that you'll ever desire.

12. ADVANCED WINNING METHODS

Several other handicapping methods deserve to be mentioned in this book. These advanced strategies should be used in conjunction with your Positional Analysis so that even more strategic numbers can be included in your Dimitrov wheels.

Skip/Hit Analysis

Numbers that have not been drawn for a long period of time are considered **overdue** and could be played. A **Skip/Hit Chart** allows you to see the exact date that each number was drawn in the lotto. With this information you can easily identify which numbers are overdue and can play them.

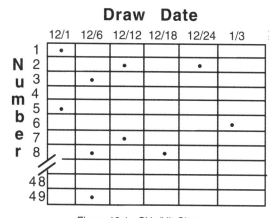

Figure 12.1 - Skip/Hit Chart

Creating a Skip/Hit Chart

In order to create your own Skip/Hit chart use a piece of paper with at least enough horizontal lines to hold each number (normally 49). Then draw vertical lines approximately 3/8 of an inch wide. This will create a space large enough to enter each number when it is drawn. Finally, include the date of each draw on the top line.

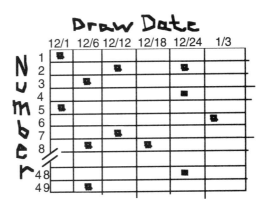

Figure 12.2 - Hand Drawn Skip/Hit Chart

According to this basic chart, numbers **1** and **5** represent the most overdue numbers because they have not been drawn since 12/1. Number **6** is the most recently drawn number and is therefore not overdue.

When using a Skip/Hit Chart you are always looking for the most overdue numbers. In lottery, these overdue numbers are often referred to as **Hot numbers** and should be compiled into a **Hot Number Chart**.* Create this chart by keeping track of the 6 most overdue or hottest numbers with the hottest one on top.

---

*In gambling, on the other hand, overdue numbers are usually referred to as **cold**.

Hot Number Chart	
Number	Draws Since Occurred
1	15
5	15
28	12
44	12
16	9
41	8

Figure 12.3 - Hot Number Chart

Prior to creating your wheels each day it is necessary to update your Hot Number Chart because the Hot Numbers can change every draw. Thus, when a number from the Hot Number Chart is drawn, it is no longer a Hot Number.

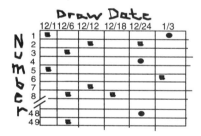

Figure 12.4 - Skip/Hit Chart with #1 Drawn

Hot Numbers with High Frequency

In order for the Skip/Hit Chart to be most effective it should be used in conjunction with a Frequency Analysis. A **Frequency Analysis** shows you how often each number has appeared in the past.

According to this strategy you are looking for numbers that have shown a high frequency over a long period of time (1 year or longer) and are also overdue. Higher frequency numbers that are overdue or **hot** make the best bets.

Hot Number Chart	
Number	Draws Since Occurred
1	15
5	15
28	12
44	12
16	9
41	8

Figure 12.5 - Hot Number Chart

In our example, **1, 5, 16, 28, 41** and **44** are the *hottest numbers*. According to the Frequency Analysis Chart (Fig. 12.6) that we analyzed, numbers **1, 5, 16** and **41** also have *high frequencies*.

Hottest Numbers:
1 5 16 28 41 44

Hot Numbers with a high frequency:
1 5 16 41

The numbers above represent hot numbers that also have a high frequency. They should definitely be included in your wheels. Add them to the chosen numbers that were previously generated in the Positional Analysis.

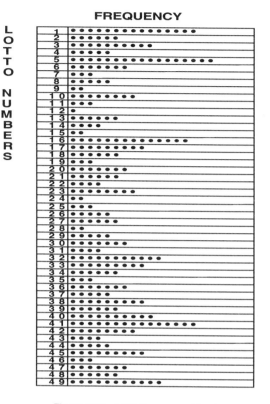

Figure 12.6 - Lotto Frequency Chart

Hot Number Chart

Number	Draws Since Occurred
1	15
⑤	15
28	12
44	12
16	9
41	8

Positional Analysis Chart

2	3	17	19	32	34
4	⑤	19	20	26	35
	7			30	
	8			31	
	9				
	14				

Figure 12.7 - Key Number Exhibited in Hot Number and Positional Analysis Charts

If a Hot Number also appears as a high frequency number from the Positional Analysis, it is considered even **Hotter**. The number **5** appears as a hot number, a high frequency number, and is also a top pick on the Positional Analysis chart. We call this a **Key Number**. (See Chapter 13 regarding Key Numbers.)

Hot Numbers with Low Frequency

This method is for players who believe that eventually all of the numbers will appear exactly the same amount of times given enough draws. The idea is similar to the *Law of Averages*.

An example would be if a coin was flipped 100 times and tails only appeared 10 times. Would tails be overdue or did heads exhibit some type of bias?

Players that believe a bias exists in the coin would play heads. Other players would choose to play tails rather than heads, because they would argue that tails was way overdue and should begin appearing much more often than heads in the future.

This *overdue* theory can also be applied to the occurrence of lotto numbers. Figure 12.8 illustrates how numbers failing to appear in the past could eventually *average out* with numbers that have already had a higher frequency of occurrence. According to this philosophy, the lower frequency numbers become the better bets.

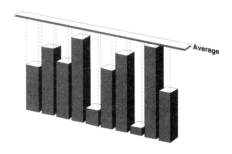

Figure 12.8 - Frequency Graph

If you believe that lower frequency numbers will appear more often in the future, then you should play low frequency instead of high frequency numbers that are on your hot number list. Below is an example of this strategy.

Hottest Numbers:
1 5 16 28 41 44

Hottest Numbers with Low Frequency:
28 44

In conclusion, I still recommend hot numbers with a high frequency over hot numbers with a low frequency, although, all hot numbers make good bets.

Cluster Analysis
In a **cluster analysis** we look at numbers that are consistently drawn together. It is not necessary to understand why these numbers are frequently paired, but playing these clusters is a good strategy.

Cluster analysis is possible only if the *actual order* of the draw can be determined. If numbers have been arranged into ascending order, it is not possible to know which numbers were actually paired.

Below are three sets of sample lotto draws in exact order of draw:

1st draw	23	14 43	02	36	43
2nd draw	33	48	04	32	22 45
3rd draw	22 45	31	09	14 43

Notice that numbers **14** and **43** clustered in the first and third draw, and **22** and **45** clustered in the second and third draw. This sample is small but it illustrates how to identify clusters.

Numbers are normally arranged into ascending order when they are listed in the newspaper. If you do not have access to the actual order of the draw, the clusters cannot be identified. Below is an example of why this is a problem.

These are the same draws sorted into ascending order:

```
02  14  13  23  36  43
04  22  32  33  45  48
09  14  22  31  43  45
```

As you can see, it is now not possible to identify the clusters. (Any clusters that occur <u>after</u> the raw numbers have been sorted into an ascending order have no meaning and should be ignored.)

Significant Cluster

A significant cluster occurs when the same number either precedes or follows another number a significant amount of times over a large group of draws.

In any group of numbers there will always be isolated instances of numbers that occur together. We are only looking for clusters that occur often enough to be considered meaningful.

In our previous example, numbers **22**, **45**, **14** and **43** represented significant clusters because they both appeared twice in the small sample. I suggest that if a cluster appears 15 times or more in 100 six ball draws, it is significant, and should be considered a cluster.

Playing A Cluster

After you have generated your chosen numbers from the Positional Analysis or Skip/Hit Chart, check them against the cluster numbers to see if you have any matches. You always include any numbers in your wheels that cluster with previous chosen numbers.

Below are the highest numbers with ties previously generated from our Positional Analysis chart (figure 6.5 on page 47).

```
   2    3   17   19   32   34
        5
        7
        8
        9
       14
```

Our clusters were **22** with **45** and **14** with **43**.

Number **14** is a top number from the Positional Analysis chart and also demonstrated significant clustering with number **43**. Number **43** should therefore be included in our wheels, along with the other chosen numbers.

If we used the highest frequency numbers from the Positional Analysis (with ties in position two), 15 chosen numbers could now be included in our wheel.

These include the 11 highest numbers from the Positional Analysis, the 4 hot numbers with high frequency (less one for the double occurrence of the number 5), and the number **43** from the cluster analysis. Below is what a Dimitrov wheeling system using our numbers would look like.

Four Guessed Numbers = 3-Number Wins

System	01	02	03	04	05	06	07	08	09	10	11	12	13	14	15
Chosen	01	02	03	05	07	08	09	14	16	17	19	32	34	41	43

Figure 12.9 - Number Bar with 15 Chosen Numbers

15/15

1	1	1	1	1	1	2	2	2	2	2	3	3	3	5
2	3	3	5	5	5	3	7	7	7	7	5	8	9	8
5	8	7	9	9	9	7	8	14	14	14	8	9	16	16
9	16	9	14	17	17	14	14	16	19	19	16	16	17	32
17	32	17	17	19	34	19	19	19	32	41	32	32	32	34
34	43	34	34	34	41	41	41	41	41	43	43	43	43	43

Figure 12.10 - Dimitrov Wheel with 15 Chosen Numbers

Charting Clusters

Understanding the theory of cluster analysis is much easier than charting it. I consider it impossible to do without the use of a computer. There are thousands of possible clusters in a 49-ball lotto and using a pencil and paper would be exhausting.

This section was designed to provide an understanding of cluster analysis for non-computer users. Computer users will be able to quickly isolate clusters and I strongly recommend that cluster strategy be incorporated into all wheels.

Regression Analysis

Regression theory has been included in this book because it is often mentioned and should be understood by both computer and non-computer users.

When the lottery commission changes the bin or adds a new set of balls, it can have a profound effect on the future numbers that are drawn. The theory behind regression analysis is that current trends can be identified if you analyze only *recently drawn numbers*.

Instead of mixing old numbers with new numbers, use draws that occurred after the date that the change happened so that the old numbers will not be included in the analysis. They will then have no effect on your predictions.

Selecting a starting point allows you to use only the most recent draws. Figure 12.11 illustrates a typical group of lotto draws. According to this example, draws older than and including 4/16 will not be used in the analysis. Draws beginning with the date 4/23, and extending to the most recent draw (shaded), will be the only numbers analyzed.

2/13	6	38	28	21	39	22
2/20	29	20	3	31	18	13
2/27	26	35	12	6	1	9
3/05	13	23	33	7	36	38
3/12	21	07	31	26	23	25
3/19	37	10	38	1	31	21
3/26	29	14	22	35	12	11
4/02	11	27	06	5	40	16
4/09	23	02	37	33	31	38
4/16	17	23	28	9	6	15
4/23	35	28	36	19	13	1
4/30	03	1	19	34	17	27
5/07	19	17	22	34	30	16
5/14	31	21	12	39	1	29
5/21	32	36	29	27	34	28
5/28	33	1	9	5	26	13
6/04	40	22	35	29	9	15

Figure 12.11- Regression of Lotto Database

Many state lottos even appear to have an optimum number of previous draws that produce the best results. In Florida, players have discovered that the last 51 draws produce the most favorable results. California handicappers use the last 26 draws to get the most wins.

Each state is different, but by using the regression analysis you can quickly identify the setting that produces the highest win percentage.

13. KEY NUMBERS

Key numbers are numbers that appear in two or more analyses. These numbers are hot and considered strategic in your betting plans. This chapter will show you how to use them to your advantage.

Positional Analysis Key Number
A double occurrence in the Positional Analysis is considered a key number.

Example of double occurrence:					
2	3	17	<u>19</u>	32	34
4	5	<u>19</u>	20	26	35
	7			30	
	8			31	
	9				
	14				

In this example, number **19** is the second highest frequency number in position #3 and the highest frequency in position #4. Because number **19** exhibited high frequency in both positions it is considered a key number.

Positional and Hot Number

If a number from the hot number chart also appears in your Positional Analysis, it should also be considered a key number.

In the hot number chart, the number 5 is listed as an overdue number. It is also a high frequency number as seen in the Positional Analysis chart. Figure 13.1 illustrates that these two factors qualify it as a key number.

Hot Number Chart	
Number	Draws Since Occurred
1	15
5	15
28	12
44	12
16	9
41	8

Positional Analysis Chart

2	3	17	19	32	34
4	5	19	20	26	35
	7			30	
	8			31	
	9				
	14				

Figure 13.1 - Hot Number Chart and Positional Analysis

Key Number Wheels

When you have key numbers it is a good idea to make sure they are in every wheel combination. Specific Dimitrov wheeling systems are designed to incorporate these key numbers.

Figure 13.2 and Figure 13.3 represent two popular Dimitrov Wheels that are designed to accept key numbers in each combination.

58: 10/27

```
0  0  0  0  0  0  0  0  0  0  0  0  0  0  0  0  0  0  0  0  0  0  0  0  0  0  0  0
1  1  1  1  1  1  1  1  1  1  1  1  1  1  1  2  2  2  2  2  2  3  3  3  3  3  3  3
2  2  2  2  2  2  2  2  2  2  4  4  4  5  6  4  4  4  4  5  6  4  4  4  4  5  6
3  3  3  3  3  3  3  3  3  4  5  5  7  7  7  5  5  5  7  7  7  5  5  5  7  7  7
4  4  4  5  5  5  6  6  6  5  6  6  8  8  8  6  6  6  8  8  8  6  6  6  8  8  8
7  8  9  7  8  9  7  8  9  6  8  9  9  9  9  7  8  9  9  9  9  7  8  9  9  9  9
```

Figure 13.2 - Dimitrov System #58

60: 11/7

```
0   0   0   0   0    0    0
1   1   1   3   3    4    6
2   2   2   4   5    7    7
3   6   8   5   8    8    8
4   7   9   6   9    9    9
5   8  10   7  10   10   10
```

Combinations (bets) are read vertically, up and down, in these charts.

Figure 13.3 - Dimitrov System #60

Unlike standard Dimitrov wheeling systems, all key number templates contain a 0 (zero) as the first system number. The key number is the chosen number that replaces the 0 in each combination.

Let's create Dimitrov Wheel #60 and learn how to use the key number in each wheel. We will use number **5** as the key number.

Five Guessed Numbers = 3-Number Wins

System	00	01	02	03	04	05	06	07	08	09	10
Chosen	05	02	03	07	08	09	14	17	19	32	34

Figure 13.4 - Dimitrov System #60 Number Bar with Chosen Numbers

60: 11/7

5	5	5	5	5	5	5
2	2	2	7	7	8	14
3	3	3	8	9	17	17
7	14	19	9	19	19	19
8	17	32	14	32	32	32
9	19	34	17	34	34	34

Figure 13.5 - Dimitrov System #60 with Chosen Numbers

If you have a key number, it is suggested that you use a key number wheel so the key number will appear in each combination. Figure 13.5 illustrates the use of Dimitrov System # 60. Notice that the key number **5** appears in each combination.

14. DREAM ANALYSIS STRATEGY

The purpose of this book is to teach you how to win the lottery using various strategies. Betting on lucky numbers, numbers associated with astrological signs or birthdays, is not a statistically valid approach. Dream analysis, while it does not use statistical analysis, is still considered by many to be a sound strategy.

This chapter will show you how to understand your dreams and use them to predict future lottery numbers.

Historical Overview Of Dream Analysis

Europeans began interpreting and analyzing their dreams early in the 16th century. They strongly believed the information derived from dreams was actually a glimpse into the future. Knowledge of the future obviously provided a tremendous amount of power so dreams were studied tenaciously.

Women were eventually designated to interpret dreams because they were considered to be more sensitive and aware than men. The practice became so widespread that European women commonly carried dream interpretation books along with their Bible in order to make correct predictions.

Gypsies were the most famous of these early prognosticators. Unfortunately, reliable dream interpretation evolved into fortune telling and eventually lost most of its former credibility. The Gypsy culture still claims to possess this ancient knowledge and continues to practice forms of prediction to this day.

Psychology And Parapsychology

Famous psychiatrists Sigmund Freud and Carl Jung also strongly believed in the power of dreams, and the minds ability to control and predict behavior through the unconscious. Freud believed that man was controlled by unconscious desires while Jung felt that the interpretation of each persons dreams was essential to mental health. They both believed that dreams symbolically represented a persons daily struggle with life.

Most recently, while earning my degree in psychology, I studied dream interpretation and other psychological and parapsychological phenomenon. Psychology refers to the study of the mind and human behavior, while parapsychology refers to the study of things like mental telepathy, mind reading and the ability to predict the future. Although it is often very difficult to prove or disprove many parapsychological phenomenon, scientists marvel at just how powerful and mysterious the human mind really is.

According to the experts, our brain uses only a small portion of its potential during conscious activity. Unconscious potential is still being explored and is thought by many to be almost unlimited. Considering that dreams reside in the unconscious, and have the potential to provide incredible insight, the interpretation of dreams and study of the mind continue to intrigue both psychic and psychologist alike.

Why You Dream

In order to interpret dreams you must first understand why you dream. During the process of dreaming your mind is actually resolving the problems and conflicts encountered while you are awake. Working through these conflicts allows your mind to reach closure so you can effectively deal with new problems. Failure to resolve these conflicts creates serious psychological problems as demonstrated in studies relating to sleep disorders.

While dreaming, a person exhibits REM (rapid eye movement) patterns. These only occur during dreams. Studies show that people who are deprived of sleep or consistently woken prior to REM patterns lose their problem solving ability and often become irrational. Researchers believe this happens because, without dreams, too many conflicts are left unresolved and therefore the mind continues to be cluttered and confused.

Dream Symbolism

Even though dreams appear to be logical and straightforward, they are actually chaotic and filled with symbolism. For the average person, the conflicts and emotions that must be resolved in their dreams are disguised and very difficult to understand. These conflicts are usually represented by a multitude of mysterious forms and symbols. But when interpreted correctly, many people believe these forms and symbols provide a glimpse into the future.

Even though the brain generates dream symbols that may be related to future events, a method is still required to associate these symbols to something that can be understood and utilized. For the purpose of winning a lottery, these symbols must obviously be associated with numbers, especially ones that are going to be selected in future draws.

Associating Dreams With Numbers

The easiest way to use your dreams as a guide to selecting winning lottery numbers is to simply match the dream symbols to the numbers they are considered to be associated with. Below are the most common symbols with their associated numbers. If a symbol in your dream is not on the chart use another symbol with similar meaning. On the following page is a sample of symbols and their associated numbers; you can find many more at your local library.

Associating Numbers With Symbols

For practice, several dream sequences will be translated into their associated numbers.

Term	No.	Term	No.	Term	No.	Term	No.
Actor	34	Cat	12, 19	Father	18	Light	37
Aircraft	2	Cattle	8	Fingers	21	Lime	43
Airport	22	Cemetery	13	Fish	17	Linen	35
Alcohol	24	Child	11	Fisherman	33	Lion	44
Altar	16	Cheese	49	Flea	47	Luggage	39
Ant	4	Chess	3	Flea market	36	Lunch	2
Antlers	31	Church	17	Flute	6		
Apple	19	Cigarette	20	Fly	20	Map	21
Apron	13	Cluster	2	Foreigner	3	Mask	45
Aquarium	4	Color	4	Furnace	33	Mushrooms	19
Artist	18	Complaint	16			Meadow	26
Aster	21	Convent	26	Garden	6	Meadow	26
Axe	15	Cotton	16	Gate	34	Military	
		Cow	21	Gift	4	service	10
Baby	1	Cucumber	48	Girl	4	Mine	31
Banquet	49	Cup	30	Gold	7	Monastery	26
Barber	37	Cut	36	Gr. mother	1	Money	27
Bars	19	Cuttler	30, 36	Grinder	23	Mother	2
Bed	38	Cyclist	3	Gypsy	40	Mother in law	5
Beggar	7	Czar	1			Mouse	46
Bell	18			Hair black	44	Murder	10
Birch	12	Dad	18	brown	29		
Blanket	17	Dagger	33	long	27	Needle	26
Boat	47	Dairy	19	white	1	Nudity	48
Book	16	Dance	48	Hammer	33		
Boy	21	Death	13	Harvest	37	Old man	1
Bread	39	Dessert	49	Hat	8	Oil	41
Bride	26	Devil	46	Heart	1		
Bridge	7	Diamond	4	Hen	21	Parents	31
Broom	2	Dinner	8	Horseshoe	4	Perfume	47
Brother	4	Dog	33	House	39	Phantom	22
Brother in law	30	Doll	3	Hunter	3	Physician	7
Bull	28	Dress (White)	7			Poison	43
Button	32	Dress (Black)	33	Inn	2	Priest	9
		Driver	8	Iron	12		
Cable	39	Drum	4			Railroad	6
Cable Car	23			Janitor	44	Rat	5
Cage	2	Earache	24			Rider	9
Candies	49	Ear-ring	28	Knife	36	Ring	19
Cap	6	Egg	13	Knot	35		
Car	14, 18	Enemy	22				
Card	7	Eye	23	Labyrinth	22		
Case	17	Fast train	1, 49	Lawyer	38		
Castle	38	Fat	29	Letter	11		

Dream #1
I dreamed that I was on an airplane that was landing. I could see a cemetery out the window. I then saw myself dead.

I dreamed that I was on an *airplane* that was *landing*. I could see a *cemetery* out the window. I then saw myself *dead*.

airplane	=	Aircraft	=	2	
landing	=	Airport	=	22	
cemetery	=	Cemetery	=	13	
dead	=	Death	=	13	(13 is a Double Occurrence.)

In this example #13 appeared twice in your dream, along with 2 and 22. These numbers could be added to your wheel, especially #13 because it was a Double Occurrence.

Dream #2
I was walking down a street. A black haired priest asked me for a cigarette and then disappeared under a bridge. I looked under the bridge and saw an old man whispering in the priest's ear and showing him a hammer.

I was walking down a street. A *black haired priest* asked me for a *cigarette* and then disappeared under a *bridge*. I looked under the bridge and saw an *old man* whispering in the priest's *ear* and showing him a *hammer*.

black hair	=	Hair Black	=	44
priest	=	Priest	=	9
cigarette	=	Cigarette	=	20
bridge	=	Bridge	=	7
old man	=	Old Man	=	1
ear	=	Earache	=	24
hammer	=	Hammer	=	33

Strategy

You have the choice to play dream-related numbers exclusively, combine them with numbers that you generated using the statistical methods previously outlined in this book, or disregard them altogether. I suggest that you use them only as bonus or extra numbers in conjunction with the numbers derived from your statistical analysis.

Conclusion

This chapter contains the basic theory of how to use dream interpretation to predict future lottery numbers. Many intelligent people believe that it works and actively use it as their only strategy. Although dream interpretation may work for many players, I believe statistical analysis is far more reliable and provides consistent winners.

15. DIMITROV WHEELS

The following chapter contains several Dimitrov wheeling systems. These wheels are designed to be used with Pick-6 lotto games. Refer to Chapter 9 for a detailed description on how to use Dimitrov Abbreviated Wheeling Systems.

Each page has a number bar at the top and selected Dimitrov Wheels. The confidence level of each wheel is displayed above the number bar. **Guessed numbers** indicate the minimum amount of chosen numbers that must be drawn for the wheel to assure you at least one winning combination. **Number wins** is the minimum win when 3, 4, or 5 of your chosen numbers match the same amount of numbers drawn.

The example below shows the number bar for a wheel that uses 14 chosen numbers. The confidence level guarantees that if 5 of your 14 chosen numbers are drawn you will have at least one 4-ball win.

Five Guessed Numbers = 4-Number Wins

System	01	02	03	04	05	06	07	08	09	10	11	12	13	14
Chosen														

The first row of numbers on the bar relates to the system numbers. These are not numbers to be played, but instead correspond to the position of your chosen numbers.

For example, 5 chosen numbers (2, 6, 7, 9, and 13) correspond to 5 system numbers in the following manner: System number 1 = chosen number 2; 2 = 6; 3 = 7; 4 = 9; and 5 =13.

The actual numbers that you place in your wheels are your chosen numbers, and are written in the blank spaces underneath the system numbers. Make sure they are arranged from lowest to highest. Once the chosen numbers have been matched with the system numbers, simply substitute the system numbers with your chosen numbers in the Dimitrov wheels.

Below is a typical Dimitrov wheeling template. The bold numbers at the top of the template describe the numeric title of the abbreviated wheeling system, how many chosen numbers it will use, and how many combinations or bets it will produce. The numbers within the template are the system numbers, and are to be substituted with your chosen numbers.

Remember, your final combinations, the actual bets you will make, will be listed vertically.

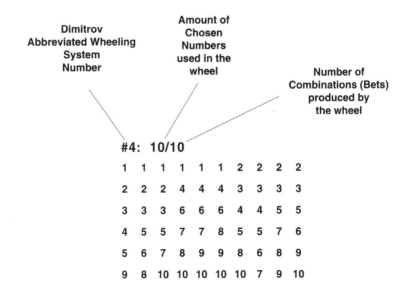

Dimitrov Abbreviated Wheeling System Number

Amount of Chosen Numbers used in the wheel

Number of Combinations (Bets) produced by the wheel

#4: 10/10

1	1	1	1	1	1	2	2	2	2
2	2	2	4	4	4	3	3	3	3
3	3	3	6	6	6	4	4	5	5
4	5	5	7	7	8	5	5	7	6
5	6	7	8	9	9	8	6	8	9
9	8	10	10	10	10	10	7	9	10

Many other valuable Dimitrov wheeling systems are available in both Prof. Jones' Lottery/Lotto Strategy Kits and Computer Software programs, which are found on pages 139-144.

Three Guessed Numbers = 3-Number Wins

System	01	02	03	04	05	06	07	08	09	10	11	12	13
Chosen													

#1: 7/4

```
1  1  1  2
2  2  2  3
3  3  3  4
4  4  5  5
5  5  6  6
6  7  7  7
```

#3: 9/7

```
1  1  1  1  1  3  4
2  2  2  2  2  5  5
3  3  3  3  6  6  6
4  4  4  4  7  7  7
5  5  5  5  8  8  8
6  7  8  9  9  9  9
```

#4: 10/10

```
1  1  1  1  1  1  2  2  2  2
2  2  2  4  4  4  3  3  3  3
3  3  3  6  6  6  4  4  5  5
4  5  5  7  7  8  5  5  7  6
5  6  7  8  9  9  8  6  8  9
9  8  10 10 10 10 10 7  9  10
```

#5: 13/21

```
1  1  1  1  1  1  1  1  1  2  2  2  2  2  3  3  3  3  4  4
2  2  2  3  3  4  4  5  5  3  3  4  4  5  5  4  4  5  5  5
3  6  10 6  7  6  7  6  10 6  8  6  8  6  7  6  7  6  7  6  10
4  7  11 8  9  8  9  7  11 7  9  7  9  9  8  9  8  9  8  7  11
5  8  12 10 11 11 10 8  12 10 12 12 10 11 10 10 11 10 11 8  12
6  9  13 12 13 12 13 9  13 11 13 13 11 12 13 13 12 13 12 9  13
```

127

Four Guessed Numbers = 4-Number Wins

System	01	02	03	04	05	06	07	08	09	10	11	12
Chosen												

#17: 7/6

```
1 1 1 1 1 2
2 2 2 2 2 3
3 3 3 3 4 4
4 4 4 5 5 5
5 5 6 6 6 6
6 7 7 7 7 7
```

#22: 12/42

```
1  1  1  1  1  1  1  1  1  1  1  1  1  1  1  1  1  1  1  1  1
2  2  2  2  2  2  2  2  2  2  3  3  3  3  3  3  4  4  4  4  4
3  3  3  3  5  5  5  7  7  9  5  5  5  6  6  6  5  5  5  6  6
4  4  4  4  6  6  6  8  8 10  7  8  8  7  7  8  7  7  8  7  9
5  7  9 11  7  9 11  9 11 11 10  9 10  9 10  9  9 10  9  9 10
6  8 10 12  8 10 12 10 12 12 12 12 11 12 11 11 12 11 11 11 12
─────────────────────────────────────────────────────────────
2  2  2  2  2  2  2  2  2  2  3  3  3  3  3  3  4  5  5  6  7
3  3  3  3  3  4  4  4  4  4  4  4  4  4  4  5  6  6  6  7  8
5  5  5  6  6  5  6  6  6  6  5  5  5  7  7  9  6  7  7  8  9
7  7  8  7  8  7  8  7  8  8  6  6  6  8  8 10  7  8  8  9 10
9 10  9  9 10  9 10 10  9 10  7 11  9  9 11 11  8  9 11 10 11
12 11 11 11 12 11 12 12 12 11  8 12 10 10 12 12  9 10 12 11 12
```

Four Guessed Numbers = 3-Number Wins

System	01	02	03	04	05	06	07	08	09	10	11	12	13	14
Chosen														

15	16	17	18

#25: 9/3

```
1 1 4
2 2 5
3 3 6
4 7 7
5 8 8
8 9 9
```

#27: 11/6

```
1 1 1 1 1  6
2 2 2 2 2  7
3 3 3 3 3  8
4 4 4 4 4  9
5 5 5 5 5 10
6 7 8 9 10 11
```

#33: 18/27

```
1  1  1  1  1  1  1  1  1  2  2  2  2  2
2  2  2  2  3  3  3  3  3  3  4  5  5  5
3  3  4  5  4  5 13 13 14  4  5 13 13 15
4  5  6  6  5  6 14 15 16  6  6 14 14 16
7  9  9 11 11  7 15 17 17 11  7 15 16 17
8 10 10 12 12  8 16 18 18 12  8 17 18 18
```

```
3  4  4  4  7  7  7  7  7  7  8  8  9
4  6  6  6  8  8  8  8  9  9  9 10 10
5 13 13 14  9  9 10 11 10 11 10 11 11
6 14 15 15 10 11 12 12 11 12 12 12 12
9 17 16 16 13 16 16 14 14 13 14 13 16
10 18 17 18 15 18 18 17 17 15 17 15 18
```

Five Guessed Numbers = 5-Number Wins

System	01	02	03	04	05	06	07	08	09	10
Chosen										

#37: 7/6

1	1	1	1	1	2
2	2	2	2	3	3
3	3	3	4	4	4
4	4	5	5	5	5
5	6	6	6	6	6
6	7	7	7	7	7

#40: 10/50

1	1	1	1	1	1	1	1	1	1	1	1	1	1	1	1	1	1	1
2	2	2	2	2	2	2	2	2	2	2	2	2	3	3	3	3	3	3
3	3	3	3	3	3	4	4	4	4	5	5	7	4	4	4	4	5	5
4	4	5	5	6	6	5	5	6	6	6	6	8	5	5	6	6	6	6
5	7	9	7	8	7	8	7	8	7	8	7	9	9	7	8	7	8	7	8
6	8	10	9	10	10	9	10	9	9	10	8	10	10	9	10	10	9	9	10

1	1	1	1	1	1	1	1	1	1	2	2	2	2	2	2	2	2	2
3	3	3	3	4	4	4	4	4	4	3	3	3	3	3	3	3	3	3
5	5	6	6	5	5	5	5	6	6	4	4	4	4	5	5	5	5	6	6
7	7	7	8	6	6	7	8	7	7	5	5	6	6	6	6	7	8	7	7
8	9	8	9	7	8	8	9	8	9	7	8	7	8	7	8	8	9	8	9
9	10	10	10	10	9	10	10	9	10	10	9	9	10	10	9	10	10	9	10

2	2	2	2	2	2	3	3	3	5
4	4	4	4	4	4	4	4	4	6
5	5	5	5	6	6	5	5	7	7
6	6	7	7	7	8	6	8	8	8
7	8	8	9	8	9	7	9	9	9
9	10	9	10	10	10	8	10	10	10

Five Guessed Numbers = 4-Number Wins

System	01	02	03	04	05	06	07	08	09	10	11	12	13	14
Chosen														

#46: 11/12

```
1  1  1  1  1  1   1   1   1   5   5   5
2  2  2  2  2  2   2   2   3   6   6   6
3  3  3  3  3  3   3   4   4   7   7   7
4  4  4  4  4  4   9   9   9   8   8   8
5  5  5  6  6  7  10  10  10   9   9  10
6  7  8  7  8  8  11  11  11  10  11  11
```

#49: 14/36

```
 1  1  1  1  1  1  1  1  1  1  1  1  1  1  1  2  2  2
 2  2  2  2  2  3  3  3  3  3  4  4  4  4  4  3  3  3
 3  5  7  9 11  5  5  5  6  6  5  5  6  6  6  5  5  6
 4  6  8 10 12  7  7  8  7  8  7  8  7  8  8  7  8  7
13 13 13 13 13  9 10  9  9 10  9 10 10  9 10  9 10 10
14 14 14 14 14 14 11 11 11 12 11 12 12 12 11 11 12 12
```
— — — — — — — — — — — — — — — — — —
```
 2  2  2  2  2  2  2  2  3  3  3  3  5  5  5  7  7  9
 3  3  4  4  4  4  4  4  4  4  4  6  6  6  8  8 10
 6  6  5  5  5  6  6  6  5  7  9 11  7  9 11  9 11 11
 8  8  7  8  8  7  7  8  6  8 10 12  8 10 12 10 12 12
 9 10 10  9 10  9 10  9 13 13 13 13 13 13 13 13 13 13
12 11 12 12 11 12 11 11 14 14 14 14 14 14 14 14 14 14
```

131

Five Guessed Numbers = 3-Number Wins

System	01	02	03	04	05	06	07	08	09	10	11	12	13	14
Chosen														

15	16	17	18	19	20	21	22	23	24	25	26	27

#55: 14/6

1	1	2	2	5	6
3	3	4	4	6	7
5	5	8	7	8	9
6	6	10	9	10	11
8	13	12	11	13	12
10	14	14	12	14	14

#49: 18/15

1	1	1	1	1	2	2	2	2	3	3	3	7	9	10
2	3	4	4	5	5	5	5	6	6	6	6	8	12	11
3	7	7	8	14	7	8	13	8	7	8	9	10	13	13
4	9	10	9	15	9	11	15	10	10	11	12	11	14	15
5	12	13	11	17	10	14	16	13	14	13	15	15	16	17
6	14	16	12	18	12	17	18	15	17	16	18	18	17	18

#64: 23/27

1	1	1	1	1	1	1	2	2	2	2	2	2	2
3	4	4	4	5	5	6	3	3	3	7	7	9	9
7	5	6	8	6	8	8	10	15	20	12	10	10	12
9	11	13	14	11	13	11	12	18	21	15	18	18	15
10	16	16	17	14	14	13	20	22	22	20	21	20	21
12	19	17	19	17	16	19	21	23	23	22	23	23	22

— — — — — — — — — — — —

3	3	3	4	4	4	4	4	5	7	7	10	11
7	7	9	5	5	8	6	6	6	9	9	12	13
10	12	10	12	6	9	8	9	8	10	15	15	14
18	15	15	18	13	11	11	11	16	12	18	18	16
21	20	21	20	14	13	14	13	17	22	20	20	17
22	23	23	22	19	17	16	17	19	23	21	21	19

Six Guessed Numbers = 5-Number Wins

System	01	02	03	04	05	06	07	08	09	10	11
Chosen											

#73: 9/9

```
1  1  1  1  1  2  3  3  4
2  2  2  2  3  4  4  5  5
3  3  3  6  5  6  6  6  6
4  4  4  7  6  7  7  7  7
5  5  5  8  7  8  8  8  8
6  7  8  9  8  9  9  9  9
```

#75: 11/27

```
1   1   1   1   1   1   1   1   1   1   1   1   1   1
2   2   2   2   2   2   2   2   3   3   3   3   4   4
3   3   3   3   4   4   5   8   4   4   5   7   5   7
4   4   5   6   5   6   6   9   5   6   6   8   6   9
5   9   8   8   10  9   8   10  7   7   7   9   7   10
6   11  11  9   11  10  10  11  11  9   8   11  10  11
```

— — — — — — — — — — — — — —

```
1   1   2   2   2   2   2   2   3   3   3   4   5
5   6   3   3   3   4   4   5   4   4   5   5   6
7   7   4   5   6   5   6   6   5   6   6   6   7
8   8   7   7   7   7   7   7   8   8   9   8   8
10  9   8   9   10  8   8   9   9   10  10  9   9
11  10  10  10  11  9   11  11  10  11  11  11  10
```

133

Six Guessed Numbers = 4-Number Wins

System	01	02	03	04	05	06	07	08	09	10	11	12	13	14	15
Chosen															

#79: 14/15

```
1   1   1   1   1   1   2   2   2   3   3   3   4   4   8
2   2   2   4   5   6   4   5   6   4   5   6   5   5  10
3   3   3   6   7   7   7   7   7   7   8   8   6   7  11
4   8  12   8   8   9   9   9   8   9   9  10   9  12  12
5  10  13   9  10  11  10  11   9  11  10  11  10  13  13
6  11  14  12  13  14  14  12  13  13  14  12  11  14  14
```

#80: 15/24

```
1   1   1   1   1   1   1   1   1   1   1   2
2   2   2   2   3   4   4   4   4   5   6   3
3   3   3   8   7   5   5   5  10   9   7   6
6   6   7  11   8   6   6   9  11  10   8   8
7  12  11  12  11   9  14  11  14  11  12  11
8  13  13  13  12  10  15  15  15  14  13  12
```
— — — — — — — — — —
```
2   2   2   2   3   3   3   4   4   5   7   7
4   4   5   6   4   5   6   5   7   6   8   9
7   9   7   7   8   8   7   6   9   9   9  11
9  10  10   8   9  10  11  10  10  11  10  13
12 14  12  11  13  13  12  12  11  14  11  14
14 15  15  13  14  15  13  14  15  15  12  15
```

134

Six Guessed Numbers = 3-Number Wins

System	01	02	03	04	05	06	07	08	09	10	11	12	13	14
Chosen														

15	16	17	18	19	20	21	22	23	24	25	26	27	28

#83: 18/9

```
 1  1  1  3  4  4  5  5  6
 2  2  2  9  6  6  8  8  7
 3  3  9 10  7  8  9 10 12
 5  7 10 11 14  9 11 12 14
13 15 11 12 16 14 13 13 16
17 17 16 17 18 18 15 15 18
```

#88: 28/36

```
 1  1  1  1  1  1  1  1  2  2  2  2  2  2  2  3  3  3
 2  3  4  4  5  5  6  6  3  3  7  9  9  9 15  4  7  9
 5  8 13 16  8 11  8 11  9 10 12 15 18 24 21 10 10 10
 6 11 14 17 13 14 14 13 10 15 20 18 21 25 24 18 20 21
 8 16 19 18 16 17 16 17 15 24 21 22 22 27 25 20 25 24
11 17 26 26 19 26 26 19 21 27 23 24 27 28 28 22 28 27
```

```
 3  3  3  4  4  4  5  5  5  6  6  7  7  8  9 12 15 21
10 10 10  5  5  6  6  7  6  7  9 12 18 11 15 18 18 22
12 12 18  8 11  8 11  8 13  8 12 15 20 13 21 22 21 23
18 23 22 14 13 13 14 11 14  9 20 20 22 14 25 23 22 24
22 25 25 17 16 17 16 19 16 10 23 23 25 16 27 25 24 25
23 28 28 19 26 26 19 26 17 11 24 27 28 17 28 28 27 26
```

16. COMPUTER STRATEGIES

Introduction

Some players ask why they would need a computer to maximize their winning chances for beating lotto and lottery games and the answer is simple: The large amount of data (previous draws) that must be stored and analyzed in order to have the best chance of winning requires the powerful resources provided by a computer.

Ever since this book and my lotto and lottery Platinum Series software were introduced, players have been asking me what kind of a computer would be sufficient to run the Prof. Jones Platinum Lotto and Lottery software. The good news is that just about any computer purchased in the last few years will be more than adequate, so have no worries on that score. Today you can purchase inexpensive systems for well under $1,000 that have significantly more power and capacity than a $50,000 super-computer system from 20 years ago.

Operating System

The "Platinum Series plus" is designed to run on Windows 95, 98, XP, probably all future Windows upgrades, and ME. This flexibility allows you to purchase an inexpensive used computer to run your program if you desire. Many Prof Jones customers, only needing a computer to run Prof Jones software, have purchased an older Pentium based laptop for under $200 and have been very happy. It ran the software perfectly and was very easy on their budget.

Lottery Software

There are many Lottery and Lotto software programs available for sale from some reputable and less reputable sources. Some of these programs have several good strategies; some have just one good strategy; while many have no strategy at all.

While of course I am biased in regards to the correct software needed to give yourself the best chance of winning a big jackpot, the Prof. Jones Platinum Series has been reviewed by many publications as being simply the most effective and best program available on the market. We put a lot of research and careful analysis into our software, and that is why so many winners have succeeded using our software, and the Platinum series is considered by many to be the best lotto and lottery software ever created.

Lottery and Lotto software programs with no strategy are simple random number generators. Considering a Lotto ticket generated by the machine at your local vendor is random, it makes little sense to spend either the money on these redundant programs, or the time generating random tickets on your own computer with these systems.

After twenty years of studying the lotto, I consider the following strategies critical in a Lottery or Lotto software program:

1. Positional Analysis.
2. Cluster Analysis.
3. Summation Analysis.
4. Dimitrov Wheeling Systems.
5. Skip/Hit charts.
6. Frequency Analysis.
7. Regression Analysis.
8. Regression Optimization.

I am not going to elaborate on the first six items on the "must-have" software list, as they are all already described in great detail throughout this book (and, of course, are included in the Prof. Jones Platinum series).

While High Frequency Numbers, Overdue Numbers, Summation Analysis and Dimitrov Wheeling Systems are very important, they are also easier to understand. Because of this, I am dedicating this section to try for once and for all, to give you an understanding of the importance of Regression Analysis in all forms of analysis.

After years of attempting to explain the more subtle aspects of winning the Lotto, I think Regression Analysis and the Optimizer are both the most important and least understood winning strategies.

The Prof Jones software line first introduced regression analysis in the NFL Football and NBA Basketball programs. Prior to using Regression Analysis, statistics (points allowed, points scored, fumbles etc.) were simply added together on a weekly basis and the aggregate was used to predict future games. This strategy would typically provide a winning percentage over the 55% level, but at the same time, in my opinion, was still woefully inadequate.

The problem with aggregate handicapping systems is that they have no way of taking recent trends into account, which are the bread and butter of handicapping. After the addition of a simple AI (artificial intelligence) Regression Analysis, the winning percentage increased by about 18%. We discovered that using the data from the last three to four football games, or the last nine to ten basketball games, dramatically increased the win percentage (*winning* in this instance, being synonymous with *beating the spread*).

The Platinum Series Lottery/Lotto software was programmed after our sports software, so we immediately added a Regression Analysis. The regression worked fine except initially the user was required to test the regressions manually. In other words, the user would set the regression at 20, 30, 40, or 60 games back, find the amount of previous data that produced the highest percentage of winners, and use this regression to predict future winning draws.

The strategy worked, but one day a customer complained that, after spending such a large sum of money on his computer, why couldn't we make the computer test the regression? That gave us something to think about so we went back to the research labs to find the optimal answer.

The Optimizer

After several months of intense work, the Optimizer was created. The Optimizer tests every possible regression (sets of previous draws) to provide the optimum regression so that it produces the highest percentage of 4, 5 and 6 ball winners. That number can then be used as the optimum Regression.

Within a month, a customer that had purchased our upgraded program (that included the Optimizer) cashed a 4.5 million dollar Lotto ticket! Need I say more about the importance of having a Regression Optimizer as part of your Lottery/Lotto arsenal?

In closing, buying the Platinum Lotto and Lottery strategies will allow you to maximize your profits.

17. BEATING KENO GAMES

Over the years, many people that are using the strategies outlined in this book have also applied them to KENO.

Although it is illegal to bring a computer or hand held device such as a Palm Pilot into the casino area, live Keno games are now being transmitted to the television screen in casino hotel rooms. The Keno player can simply use the phone to place a bet. The bet is added to the room bill in the same way as food or beverage. The good news is that you can finally track previous draws; the bad news is that you do not receive any complimentary drinks! (On my most recent visit to Las Vegas I simply purchased the beverage of my choice in the Casino lobby, went up to my room and fired up my computer.)

Considering Regression Analysis is not a necessary strategy for Keno, it is possible to enhance your win percentage using methods outlined in this book without the aid of a computer. But as I have already noted, access to a computer and a viable software program makes it so much faster, and you can actually enjoy the experience.

Keno Structure
Keno consists of a display board containing 80 numbers (1-80), 20 of which are randomly drawn over the course of the game. The bet consists of predicting as many of the 15 numbers drawn as possible. Most Keno games allow bets on as few as one to three numbers as the minimum wager, and up to 15 numbers as the maximum wager.

To date, the maximum 15 out of 15 Keno bet has never actually been won. Although it was "won" one time, the winner spent two years in prison along with the computer programmer that rigged the game. The reason they were caught is because the 15-15 prize is essentially "impossible" to win, so the casino knew something was wrong.

Like the Lottery, the top prize pays a lot of money, but the odds of picking 15 correct numbers out of a 20 number draw from a pool of 80 numbers is astronomical and especially designed for "suckers."

Due to the odds, but more importantly, the fact that 99.9% of the players use no strategy when choosing their numbers, Keno is one of the most profitable games for the casino. The game is readily available in most places in the casino - you will even find Keno cards on many dinner tables. "Birthdays" actually dominate the bulk of Keno strategy for most players.

Keno Strategy

Considering the large pool of potential numbers (80), many of the strategies outlined in this book are simply not feasible. For example, it would take at least four games for all numbers to "possibly" be drawn (obviously some numbers will not be drawn, which is actually the strength of your strategy).

Such a large pool of numbers makes strategies such as Regression and Positional Analysis impossible, but the following Lotto strategies can effectively be used for Keno.

Best Lotto Strategies To Use For Keno

In order to use the Lotto strategies to play Keno, first create a "file," entering 20 drawn numbers out of the 80 number pool. This can be done by hand using this book in conjunction with the Master Strategy Kit, but due to the massive amount of data, a computer and Lottery software program is strongly suggested. Considering that the Summation Analysis is very important, doing it "live" by hand would almost be impossible.

Hot numbers (numbers that are overdue) are typically the numbers used in your "playable number" list. I refer to "list" because Keno requires you to use several strategies together.

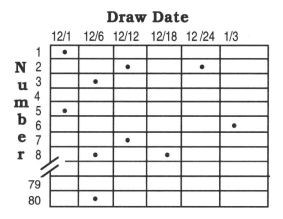

The basic strategy is to derive the 20-30 "Hot" numbers from the Skip/Hit Chart, and then use a Summation Analysis to get rid of the numbers that contain too many high or low numbers. These chosen numbers then get applied to the appropriate 5 Ball Dimitrov Wheeling System. This will narrow you down to 6-10 quality bets.

Minimum Number Of Games Required

You will need to enter (by hand or computer) a "minimum" of 10 complete Keno games prior to making any type of bet. Plan on spending some time before you have enough data necessary to make your first bet.

Winning with Overdue Numbers

You are looking for "Hot Numbers," numbers that have not yet been drawn, or numbers that have possibly been drawn only one time. If a random number generator is used to select the numbers, finding a bias (as in Lotto) would be quite difficult, if not outright impossible. If the Keno game is in fact using balls, as is typical in most casinos, then a bias is possible, and strategies other than Hot Numbers would be viable. In these cases, you would then play Keno exactly like Lotto

For this discussion, we will assume random numbers are being generated by a computer, so overdue numbers are the most meaningful. If, for example, 400 numbers have been drawn out of a pool of 80 and there are still numbers that have not appeared, these are the numbers that are "most likely" to be drawn, even though it is random. I suggest that you use your Skip/Hit Chart and select all of the numbers that have not been drawn, or have been drawn only one time. Then, apply a reasonably tight Summation Analysis to reduce the numbers to a manageable amount and play the remaining numbers.

If you have the patience to enter 1000 or more numbers you would then be able to throw High Frequency numbers into your plays.

KENO STRATEGY

1. Skip/Hit Chart - Last 30-40 numbers chosen either one time or never.

2. Summation Analysis to reduce the numbers down to a reasonable amount.

3. Using either a Dimitrov Wheel or every permutation of the numbers, bet them in sets of no more than 5 numbers. DO NOT play more than 5 numbers in a single bet.

4. High Frequency Numbers are viable if 1000 or more numbers are entered into the database.

I cannot stress enough that Keno players play no more than the "5" picks per card for the best odds. For example, if you have 15 numbers that are overdue and have also passed the Summation Analysis test, DO NOT go to the window and bet that you can pick 15 out of 15. Use Dimitrov Wheels to break the numbers into 5 Ball groups and play them as individual bets.

A second option would be to create "every" permutation of the 15 numbers and bet them in blocks of 5. This would actually guarantee the win if even 5 of your numbers came in, something the Dimitrov Wheels couldn't do. (A sample 5 Number Keno ticket is shown on the following page.)

I strongly suggest you read use the advanced strategies in the back of this book to give yourself every chance of winning not only at lotto and lottery games, but also at keno.

Be a winner!

1—

5

1	2	3	4	✗	6	7	8	9	10
11	✗	13	14	15	16	17	18	19	20
21	22	23	24	25	26	27	✗	29	30
31	32	33	34	35	36	37	38	39	40

KENO LIMIT $50,000.00 TO AGGREGATE PLAYERS EACH GAME

41	42	43	44	45	46	47	48	49	50
51	52	53	54	✗	56	57	58	59	60
61	✗	63	64	65	66	67	68	69	70
71	72	73	74	75	76	77	78	79	80

WINNING TICKETS PAID IMMEDIATELY AFTER EACH KENO GAME

KENO RUNNERS ARE AVAILABLE FOR YOUR CONVENIENCE
WE ARE NOT RESPONSIBLE IF TICKETS ARE TOO LATE FOR CURRENT GAME

146

18. FINAL WORD

After reading this book you will be able to play any lottery or lotto with excellent results. We've shown you how to create wheels that utilize all of your top Positional Analysis and hot numbers and how to identify and incorporate key numbers in a winning strategy.

To further your winning chances, non-computer users should also consider the master Strategy kits discussed in the back of this book. These kits will provide you with many hard to find Dimitrov wheeling systems and other essential templates and information. Not only are they a good buy, but they also make the strategies easier to follow and chart.

Computer users will be thrilled with the Platinum Series software listed in the back of this book. This software, which is the most powerful winning lotto and lottery software ever made, makes difficult strategies like the cluster and regression analysis a snap. Combining the knowledge of this book with the power of your computer creates a powerful combination.

Whether you use just the book, or you decide to expand your arsenal with either the powerful Master Strategy kits or computer software, you'll now have the odds on your side and the power to win the big jackpot!

19. GLOSSARY OF TERMS

Abbreviated Wheeling System - System used to create betting combinations that do not contain every permutation of the numbers wheeled.

Assurance- Guaranteed win in an abbreviated wheeling system that occurs when the minimum number of chosen numbers are drawn.

Bell Curve - A statistical model used to illustrate distribution of numbers.

Best Number Analysis - The determination of the highest frequency number in a particular statistical analysis.

Best Number/Digits - Most frequently drawn number/digit.

Bias - When an event occurs more often than normally occurs randomly.

Bonus Ball - A lotto ball selected after the initial draw that can be used to create a winning ticket.

Box - Betting combinations of numbers as a group.

Chosen Numbers - Actual numbers used in betting wheels.

Cluster Analysis - The analysis of numbers drawn together frequently enough to be considered significant.

Combinations - The product of wheels that represent the actual bets.

Complete Wheeling System - A system used to create betting combinations that contain every permutation of the numbers wheeled.

Confidence Level - Guaranteed assurance in an abbreviated wheeling system that occurs when the minimum number of chosen numbers are drawn.

Digit - An individual number ranging from 0 to 9.

Dimitrov Wheeling System - An abbreviated method of wheeling six numbers that does not contain all permutations but still maintains an assurance of winning.

Dream Interpretation - Understanding relationships between dream symbols and their associated numbers.

Fixed Prize - A method of lotto payoff that offers prizes of a predetermined amount of money.

Frequency - The percentage of occurrence relating to an event or number.

Frequency Analysis - An analysis of the number or percentage of occurrences relating to events or numbers.

Guessed Numbers - The minimum amount of chosen numbers necessary for a guaranteed win in an abbreviated wheeling system.

Hot Number - The numbers most overdue for selection. Commonly associated with the Skip/Hit Chart.

Instant Games - Scratch-off lottery games that offer a fixed prize and require no strategy.

Key Numbers - Numbers that appear in two or more analyses and should be played in all wheels.

Lottery - Games that select 3 or 4 balls out of individual pools containing balls numbered from 0 to 9. Games typically pay 50% of the pool.

Lotto - Games that select from 5 to 20 numbers out of a single pool and offer million dollar top prizes.

Lotto Sum - The process of adding all the numbers in a betting combination.

Number Bar - Bar containing system and chosen numbers in a paired format.

Order of Draw - The sequence that balls are drawn. In lottery it creates the actual number (4201) and is important. In lotto it is of no consequence.

Overdue - A number that has not been drawn over a period of time.

Pick Four - A lottery that selects 4 balls drawn from independent pools with a digit range of 0 to 9. Numbers can contain duplicate digits.

Pick Three - A lottery that selects 3 balls drawn from independent pools with a digit range of 0 to 9. Numbers can contain duplicate digits.

Positional Digit Analysis - An evaluation of the frequency of order that each digit is drawn in a lottery.

Power Ball - A lotto game that involves selecting 5 balls from one pool and the 6th ball (Power Ball) from a different pool; the Power Ball itself.

Regression Analysis - The process of analyzing a more recent portion of a database in order to increase the win percentage.

Secondary Prize - Any lottery or lotto prize that is not the Top Prize.

Significant Cluster - Two numbers occurring together often enough so as to be deemed significant.

Skip/Hit Analysis - A time oriented analysis indicating the exact date each ball is drawn. It is used to determine the most overdue or "Hot" numbers.

Straight Bet - A one-ticket bet.

Sum Total Analysis - The process of adding up all of the numbers in each combination of a wheel. High and low totals that rarely occur can then be identified and eliminated from the bet.

System Numbers - A wheeling system number pattern often referred to as a template. Chosen numbers are paired with system numbers to create betting combinations.

Target Range - The range in a Sum Total Analysis that contains 85% or higher of the winning combinations. Often associated with a Bell Curve.

Template - The wheeling system number pattern. (See System Numbers).

Top Prize - The highest or first prize in a lottery or lotto

Wheeling System - A method of including more numbers into a bet than the amount of numbers necessary for a single combination. A wheel is necessary when more than 6 numbers are played in a 6 ball lotto.

Variable Prize - A method of lotto payoff that offers prizes based on the pool and number of winning tickets.

Platinum "PLUS" Lottery/Lotto™ charts

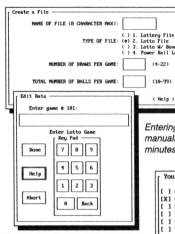

The Platinum Series "Plus" Lottery/Lotto™ program allows you to play any kind of lottery or lotto game. You can play 3 or 4 number lottery, or any style lotto including bonus or power balls. Play any number of lotteries and lottos, your only limitation is the size of your hard drive.

Entering your game data is simple and quick. Type in the numbers manually or use your mouse for the built-in key pad. A couple of minutes a week is all it takes to keep your game files up-to-date.

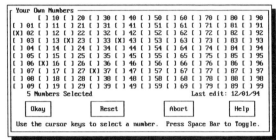

You aren't limited to playing numbers that the program picks. Whether they're lucky numbers, birthdays or numbers that match up from several types of analysis, you can quickly create *your* combinations. Just 'click' the numbers and create the wheels.

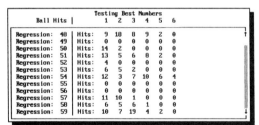

Regression Testing finds the most productive regression settings. The regression setting determines how much game history to use in the analysis. For example, does using 50 of the previous games give better results than 100? In this example you can see that 54 is the best regression setting since it gives the highest number of 4, 5 and 6-ball hits.

Lotto Sum Analysis is a technique used by professional lotto handicappers to eliminate combinations of numbers that have a very low frequency of occurrence. From the chart you can see how very low sums (below 65) and very high sums (above 233) have never occurred during the past 500 games. With Lotto Sums these wheels are automatically removed in order to optimize your bet.

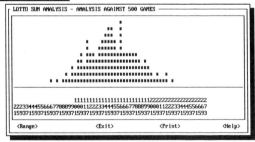

Use the installed wheeling systems or your own Custom Systems to wheel your numbers. The Platinum "Plus" Lottery/Lotto™ then **optimizes** these combinations to help you win the most amount of money with the fewest number of bets.

Use Ordering Coupon on following page
or charge by phone (800)577-WINS

PLATINUM "PLUS" LOTTERY/LOTTO™

Prof. Jones' Pro Level Computer Strategy - **For Serious Players**(IBM and Mac)

NEW REVISION! - The **king** of Lottery/Lotto software has gotten even better! New revision includes Power Ball, Summation Analysis/Charts, Last Number Recall, Wheel Optimizer. Use this super-powerful and versatile system to play and beat 3 and 4 number lottery; five ball, six ball, power ball or bonus ball lottos. Unique user-friendly "click and pick" creates scientific wheels quick and easy - let the program do the work! Only lotto program featuring **Artificial Intelligence!!!** The Platinum Plus includes all the goodies of the Mini-Platinum Plus **and more**, and is for players **going for the max!!!**

SUPER STRATEGY - This **super strategy** features **over 20** of the Dimitrov Systems, the Hard Positional Analysis, all the Cluster, Bell, % of Occurrence, % of Frequency, Past Winning Numbers, Two Digit Numbers and lots more!

MORE FEATURES! - This **awesome** strategy features an **expanded** cluster analysis, skip/hit chart, **hot number** & regression analysis/testing, *unlimited* wheeling systems! **Very powerful**, excellent **top-of-the-line** strategy! Includes hardbound manual, 90 day after-purchase support & replacement warranty with optional 1 year extension, and is backed by more than **ten years of customer satisfaction**!

To order, send $149.95 by check or money order to:
Cardoza Publishing, P.O. Box 1500, Cooper Station, New York, NY 10276

FIVE BALL LOTTO WHEELS
Prof. Jones' Winning Strategy for Non-Computer Users

SPECIAL 5-BALL STRATEGY PACKAGE

For **5-ball lotto players**, this special package **gives you the master strategy** five ball wheels that allow you to play your **best numbers** and go for the big wins that other players dream about! **Popular and powerful**, these wheels get you ready for the action.

30 WHEELS INCLUDED

A **wide variety of wheels** covers bets for all situations, from **5 game plays** with a variety of best numbers, to wheels covering **24 game plays**, and others covering more than 20 of best number picks.

You'll find wheels such as 7 numbers-12 plays (7/12), 11/3, 19/18, 6/6 and 25 more great wheeling combinations to cover all your needs.

OTHER FEATURES

The 5-Ball Lotto Wheels Strategy Kit also contains **20** 5-Ball Lotto Sum Templates, a **clear Template** for ease-of-use in wheeling your best numbers, and a **5-Ball Lotto Sum chart** to provide a range of numbers and a guide in number-choosing strategies to help you win.

BONUS - Wheeling instructions included!

To order, send $25 by check or money order to: **Cardoza Publishing**

159

Pro-Master II Lotto and Lottery Strategies

- Prof. Jones' Ultimate Winning Strategy For Non-Computer Users -

Finally, after years of research into winning lotto tickets, Prof Jones has developed the ultimate in **winning jackpot strategies** for non-computer users! This **new powerhouse** gives you the **latest** in winning lotto strategies!

EASY TO USE - MINUTES A DAY TO WINNING JACKPOTS!

These **scientific winning systems** can be used successfully by anyone! Spend only **several minutes a day** inputting past winning numbers into the master templates and this **amazing system** quickly and **scientifically** generates the numbers that have the **best chances** of making you rich.

THE MASTER LOTTO/LOTTERY STRATEGIES AND MORE!

All the goodies of the Master Lotto/Lottery strategies - the winning systems, instruction guides, clear working template and bonus templates - are included in this **powerful winning strategy**, plus such **extra** features as the 3-Ball, 4-Ball and 6-Ball Sum Total charts. You also receive...

100 WHEELING SYSTEMS

That's right, **100** advanced Dimitrov Wheeling Systems - **double** the systems of the excellent Master Lotto/Lottery package! You'll be using the **most powerful** lotto and lottery winning systems ever designed.

BONUS

Included **free** with this **super strategy** are 15 Positional Analysis templates, 10 each 3-Ball, 4-Ball and 6-Ball Sum Total Templates and 15 Best Number templates!

EXTRA BONUS

Order now and you'll receive, **absolutely free** with your order, the extra bonus, 7 Insider Winning Tips - a conside guide to **extra winning strategies**!

$50.00 Off! This $99.95 strategy is now only $49.95 with this coupon!

To order, send ~~$99.95~~ $49.95 plus postage and handling by check or money order to:
Cardoza Publishing, P.O. Box 1500, Cooper Station, New York, NY 10276

$50 OFF!!! (with this coupon) Win Big Money Jackpots!

Yes! Please rush me Prof. Jones **Pro-Master II Lotto and Lottery Systems**. Enclosed is a check or money order for ~~$99.95~~ $49.95 (plus postage and handling) to:
Cardoza Publishing
P.O. Box 1500, Cooper Station, New York, NY 10276
MC/Visa/Amex orders can be placed by phone at (800)577-WINS

Please include $5.00 postage and handling for U.S. & Canada, other countries $10.00. Orders outside United States, money order payable in U.S. dollars on U.S. bank only.

NAME _____

ADDRESS _____

CITY _____ STATE _____ ZIP _____
MC/Visa/Amex Orders By Mail

MC/Visa # _____ Phone _____

Exp. Date _____ Signature _____

Order Now! 30 Day Money Back Guarantee!   LO 160

160